Challenging
Motherhood(s)

Pearson
Education

We work with leading authors to develop the
strongest educational materials in sociology,
bringing cutting-edge thinking and best learning
practice to a global market.

Under a range of well-known imprints, including
Prentice Hall, we craft high-quality
print and electronic publications which help
readers to understand and apply their content,
whether studying or at work.

To find out more about the complete range of our
publishing please visit us on the World Wide Web at:
www.pearsoneduc.com

Challenging Motherhood(s)

Julie A. Wallbank

Lancaster University

An imprint of **Pearson Education**

Harlow, England · London · New York · Reading, Massachusetts · San Francisco · Toronto · Don Mills, Ontario · Sydney
Tokyo · Singapore · Hong Kong · Seoul · Taipei · Cape Town · Madrid · Mexico City · Amsterdam · Munich · Paris · Milan

Pearson Education Limited
Edinburgh Gate
Harlow
Essex CM20 2JE
England

and Associated Companies throughout the world

Visit us on the World Wide Web at:
http://www.pearsoneduc.com

First published 2001

ISBN 0 130 87399 3

British Library Cataloguing-in-Publication Data
A catalogue record for this book is available from the British Library

Library of Congress Cataloging-in-Publication Data
Wallbank, Julie A.
  Challenging motherhood(s) / Julie A. Wallbank
      p. cm.
  Includes bibliographical references and index.
  ISBN 0-13-087399-3
    1. Mothers—Social conditions. 2. Motherhood. I. Title.
  HQ759.W315 2000
  306.874'3—dc21   00–063692

10 9 8 7 6 5 4 3 2 1
05 04 03 02 01

Typeset by 35 in 9/13.5 pt Stone Serif
Produced by Pearson Education Asia Pte Ltd.
Printed in Malaysia

For Danny Winder with love. Thank you for allowing me the space to write this book and for understanding and acknowledging that I am more than 'mother'.

contents

author's acknowledgements

I should like to extend my deepest gratitude to the many people who assisted me in the preparation of this book: above all to the women who participated in the interviews and who gave and entrusted me with some of the most intimate details of their lives. Without their generosity this project would not have been possible. I am also greatly indebted to the various wonderful people who influenced and continue to inspire me and support my work: Alison Young, Peter Rush, Michael Salter, Celia Lury, Leslie Moran, Katherine O'Donovan and Richard Collier. I am fortunate to be able to count them as respected peers and friends. They have all offered their own distinctive brands of encouragement and guidance.

Special thanks also to Beverley Skeggs of Manchester University and Jane Fortin of the Law Faculty at King's College, London, for their valuable comments and insights into my work. I am also grateful to the academic and supportive environment provided by members and former members of the Law Department at Lancaster University; particularly influential have been Leslie Moran, Elena Loizidou, Michael Salter, Alison Young, Peter Rush, Sarah Beresford, David Seymour, Mike MacNair, Piyel Haldar, Marinos Diamantedes, Costas Douzinas and Peter Goodrich. I am also grateful to the Department and the Faculty of Social Sciences for giving me the space to write.

During the book's production I suffered from the sad deaths of my mother Phoebe Wallbank, my brother Ronnie Wallbank and my uncle, Jimmy Harris. I must extend my deepest thanks and love to Elena Loizidou for helping me through these most awful times. There are personal friends too numerous to permit a comprehensive list who supported me throughout the preparation and writing of this book. A few do need special mention: Glen Hodgetts for being my undergraduate intellectual sparring partner, Alan Dickinson, Christine Hornby, Moira Maher, Michelle Hodgson, Lisa Parker, Paul and Karen Hegarty, and Louise Roberts. I also thank all my friends in Leeds, Nottingham and London and especially the Bridlington group – you know who you are! I am also grateful to 'the Grandy's', 'the Baines's' and Jan Nicholson for their continuing love.

My friend, student and research assistant Caroline Jones deserves special attention for providing abundant enthusiasm and practical assistance on this and other projects. Without her the task would have been lonelier and more arduous and I extend the deepest gratitude. I am also indebted to my students for allowing me to try out new ideas, particularly, LLM Law and the Body 1999–00, Gender and the Law 1998–99 (especially Sarah Jane Solomon) and Children and the Law 1998–99 & 00.

My thanks also go to Neil Grandy, who lived with me during the period of the preparation of this book and provided its backing music. Belated thanks to Phoebe Wallbank for her valuable practical support.

The research for this book was generously funded by the British Academy.

publisher's acknowledgements

We are grateful to the following for permission to reproduce copyright material:

Guardian News Service Limited for the headlines 'Tripled maintenance payments led to divorcee's death' from THE GUARDIAN 7.12.93, 'No need for a man about the house' from THE GUARDIAN 2.7.94, 'CSA letter caused suicide' in THE GUARDIAN 25.11.94 and 'CSA delaying father's appeals' in THE GUARDIAN 15.12.94; Independent Newspapers Limited for the article 'Fathers who are treated as paupers' by Angela Neustatter from THE INDEPENDENT 19.9.93; Kluwer Academic Publishers for extracts from the articles 'An unlikely match? Foucault and the lone mother' by Julie Wallbank from LAW & CRITIQUE Volume IX No. 1 1998 and 'Social and legal responses to women who renounce men' by Julie Wallbank from LIVERPOOL LAW REVIEW Volume XX (2) 1998; the author Liz Lochhead for the poem 'Everybody's Mother' from THE VIRAGO BOOK OF WICKED VERSE; Sage Publications for the article 'The campaign for change of the child support act 1991: reconstituting one absent father' by Julie Wallbank from SOCIAL & LEGAL STUDIES Vol XI No. 2 © Sage Publications 1997; Society of the Public Teachers of Law for an extract from the article 'Returning the subject to the subject of women's poverty' by Julie Wallbank from LEGAL STUDIES Volume III No. 2 and Taylor and Francis for an extract from the article 'Castigating mothers: the judicial response to wilful women in disputes over paternal contact in English law' by Julie Wallbank from JOURNAL OF SOCIAL WELFARE & FAMILY LAW Volume 20 No. 4 1998 – http://www.tandf.co.uk/journals.

Theorizing mothers:
a Foucauldian approach

Everybody's Mother

Of course,
everybody's mother always and
so on . . .
Always never
loved you enough
or too smothering much.
Of course you were the Only One, your
mother
a machine
that shat out siblings, listen
everybody's mother
was the original Frigid-
aire Icequeen clunking out
the hardstuff in nuggets, mirror
silvers and ice-splinters that'd stick
in your heart
Absolutely everyone's mother
was artistic when she was young.
Everyone's mother
was a perfumed presence with pearls, remote
white shoulders when she
bent over in her ball dress
to kiss you in your crib.
Everybody's mother slept with the butcher

for sausages to stuff you with.
Everyone's mother mythologised herself. You got mixed up
between dragon's teeth and blackmarket stockings.
Naturally
she failed to give you
Positive Feelings
about your own sorry
sprouting body (it was a bloody shame)
but she did
sit up all night sewing sequins
on your carnival costume
so you would have a good time
and she spat
on the corner of her hanky and scraped
at your mouth with sour lace till you squirmed
so you would look smart
And where
was your father all this time?
Away
at the war, or
in his office, or any-
way conspicuous for his
Absence, so
what if your mother did
float around above you
big as a barrage balloon
blocking out the light?
Nobody's mother can't not never do nothing right.

(Lochhead 1984)

Liz Lochhead's poem is used here to describe the ambivalent position of lone mothers in contemporary discourses on the lone mother headed
household generally and on the politically hot issue of child support more
specifically. On the one hand, lone mothers are constructed in recent social,
legal and political debates as being unable to raise children adequately
alone yet on the other hand when a relationship ends it is still expected
that women will provide children with their day-to-day care. Moreover,
they also become obliged to provide for their children in a financial sense
if the estranged father refuses to do so and when the state demonstrates
a reluctance to provide. Lochhead's poem reflects the manner in which
mothers generally are simultaneously vilified and revered. In many of the

popular discourses on lone motherhood, particularly during the early 1990s, lone mothers are denied any reverence, the emphasis being upon the constructed failings of the lone mother. During the first years of the 1990s, lone mothers were subjected to a great deal of vilification in the press coverage of the post-separation family, the Child Support Act 1991 and in debates about 'the family' and lone motherhood more generally. In social and legal discourse, lone mothers were often constructed as the scourge of society for their alleged drain on public resources and for the alleged threat that they posed to the nuclear family, traditional masculine roles therein and to society as a whole. Political debates about lone motherhood, the post-separation family, non-residential fathers and the issue of child support were generated during a time in which 'the hegemony of the theory of the underclass . . . is one of the triumphs of the New Right' (Campbell 1993: 306). According to Campbell, the underclass theorists provided a name for all the people who disrupted Britain in the 1990s. Lone mothers or 'single' mothers (as popularly known) were regarded as part of the underclass. Lone mothers were held responsible for the decline in the traditional nuclear family. Women were seen as engineering the expulsion of fathers from the home for the sake of their own independence, even though their independence from men was likely to mean their living in impoverished conditions.[1] However, like Lochhead's 'Mother', the lone mother of contemporary discourse is relied upon to fulfil all her children's needs in the face of the non-presence of the father.

Political debates about the financial maintenance of children in the post-separation context constructed child support as a problem that was desperately in need of resolution. The government used statistical information to establish the extent of the problem of the growing number of lone mothers who were dependent upon the state for support. Statistics were also used to tell a 'truth' about the extent of the phenomenon that fathers were failing to provide for their children after the end of an adult relationship. The family was targeted as the best means of solving the 'problem'. The first Child Support Act 1991, implemented in April 1993, was introduced in order to make more fathers pay for the financial maintenance of their children than had been the case under the previous system. The Act established a public body, the Child Support Agency, to enforce the legislation. I examine the socio-political context in which child support legislation was introduced, and I also consider the then Conservative government's alleged intended trajectories for the Act as outlined in the original White Paper (HMSO 1990). I argue that one aim was given

---

1. See, for example, Dennis and Erdos 1992.

priority both in the legislation and in the enactment of the new law over and above the government's other stated aims. That overriding aim was to reduce social security expenditure and to make fathers pay. I will show that the desired attainment of this single objective determined how lone mothers and non-residential fathers were constructed in social, political and legal discourse during the early 1990s.

For example, the then Conservative government stressed that there was a 'public interest' in ensuring that fathers remain financially responsible for their children. Within the discourse of a public interest, the taxpaying two-parent family was used as an example of being more deserving of public support than the lone mother headed household. I will show how lone parent families have been constructed and indeed continue to be constructed as being deviant units and not real families at all, and that as such they are constructed as less deserving than their two-parent counterparts. While the Child Support Act was predominantly concerned with ensuring that the financial link between fathers and their children is maintained in the post-separation context, it also, along with a variety of other social and legal discourses, established normative guidelines of appropriate maternal and paternal behaviour in the post-separation context.

Like Lochhead's 'absent' father, non-residential fathers of contemporary discourses on child support were similarly constructed as 'absent' and also therefore as problematic. Using a number of legal contexts, I will show that legal discourse draws upon the knowledge of other discourses in order to promote the idea that father presence and participation is good for the family and for society as a whole. I will demonstrate that because of the widespread acceptance that the family and society benefits from father participation lone mothers are expected to ensure that they incorporate a father into their children's lives. In Chapter 4, I focus on the context of child support and show how much of the press coverage constructed non-residential fathers as feckless and as distant and uninvolved in family life. The perceived disconnection of men from the realm of the familial is rendered problematic within a number of discourses, including those of the academic disciplines of sociology, criminology, men's studies and gender studies. I show how these discourses are used by law in order to ensure as far as is possible the continuing connection between fathers and their children, even in situations that have the potential to threaten the well-being of the child involved.

Additionally, I argue that due to the way that fathers' rights arguments have gained prominence in recent years, not any father will do. That is to say, providing a child with a social father does not mean that the biological father is rendered redundant. Chapter 3 focuses upon the

issue of paternal contact in the post-separation context. Through an analysis of Court of Appeal decisions I show how judges are strongly influenced by the perceived desirability of continuing parent/child relations. The
law is concerned to return the father back to the family and to place him
inside rather than marginal or Other to the familial realm. Lone mothers
who are viewed as wilfully renouncing biological fathers can expect to meet
with a good deal of social and legal disapprobation.

I also demonstrate how mothers are defined through an articulation
of their children's needs. Moreover, I argue that in debates about what
children need there is no accompanying discussion of the needs of the
mother. A lone mother's needs become occluded by the needs of her children. The story of the post-separation family is also told through data collected from nine interviews with lone mothers. I am concerned with giving
a voice to at least some of the lone mothers who have been constituted
in the mainstream discourses, for their own knowledge and experiences
have largely been marginalized or disqualified by those discourses that have
constructed their subjectivities. I aim to show how lone mothers make sense
of and negotiate their lives within and through the network of power relations as disseminated through discourse.

Foucault's theory of discourse

According to Foucault, the modern subject is constituted by culturally and historically specific discourses. Discourse is defined as the
'manifold relations of power which permeate, characterise and constitute
the social body' and which are disseminated throughout the population
(Foucault 1980: 93).

Discourses are extremely potent and they function by producing certain truths. To use an example taken from this project, it has been posited
that children suffer psychological damage as a result of a lack of paternal
contact. This statement, generated by a psychological framework, effectively
lays down a scientific claim to know that the child who suffers paternal
deprivation may turn out to be a damaged individual. The postulation that
harm will be suffered by the child through paternal lack effectively places
the child and her or his family in the network of power generated by that
discourse as the family is constructed as a site of potential problems.

Discourse therefore establishes a set of rules that may or may not
be adhered to by individuals. Families may or may not choose to ensure
ongoing paternal contact, but in the event that the child is constructed
as damaged in some way the family that does not ensure paternal contact

will be seen as falling outside the normative framework laid down by the psychological discourse. The family may then be treated as in need of some form of psychological or social modification. Discourses transmit and produce both power and truth, and as Foucault says: 'We are subjected to the production of truth through power and we cannot exercise power except through the production of truth' (*ibid.*).

With respect to the issue of truth, Foucault's analysis is not concerned with uncovering that which is propounded as true; rather it is concerned with examining the manner in which the power/knowledge formulation operates at the level of the micro-social in order to produce regimes of truth. Foucault denounces the adoption of the grand theory of modernity in favour of small-scale studies that focus upon how power is experienced and exercised in specific situations. He asserts that modern power must be construed as 'capillary' and that it has to be analysed at the lowest extremities of social life in everyday social practices (*ibid.*: 96). Foucault's own studies focused upon how power is exercised in the apparatuses of surveillance in prisons, in the medicalization of sexuality and of madness and criminality. Foucault has also stated that he is not interested in identifying *who* is responsible for the wielding of power against repressed groups. In fact, he goes so far as to say that no one person or group *holds* power over another. Instead, he is interested in the effects of power and knowledge that discourses ensure and what makes the use of these discourses necessary.

Foucault and normalization

In defining the Foucauldian concept of discourse, it is necessary to consider the related concept of normalization. Much of Foucault's work was taken up with the operation of power through normalizing practices and techniques. He argued that modern forms of government increasingly operate on the basis of the management of the population through normalizing techniques rather than through coercion. He suggested that the new domains of knowledge, for example in the fields of psychology and sociology, set down normative rules that came to supplant the rule of the law in regulating human behaviour. However, Carol Smart has challenged the extent to which this has occurred (1989: 8).

Normalization operates by setting up a norm to which individuals must conform. Individuals are measured and judged according to how closely they conform to the desired norm. The effect of the normalizing judgement is to establish a standard of behaviour towards which everyone is encouraged. Any individual behaviour that falls outside what has been defined and valued as normal is marginalized and is perceived as in need of modification.

Consequently, normalizing power imposes a homogeneous standard of behaviour to which each individual is directed. According to this formulation, normalizing judgement is simultaneously individualistic and homogeneous as it seeks to make individuals conform to the acceptable standard of behaviour. It is a form of 'perpetual penality . . . it traverses all points and supervises every instant in the disciplinary institutions, compares, differentiates, hierarchises, homogenises, excludes. In short, it normalises' (Foucault 1977: 183). Conformity to the norm is the goal, and non-conformity will be sanctioned. In their attempts to attain the norm, individuals self-regulate according to prevailing normative practices. Thus, the dominant forms of subjectivity are maintained through the individual's self-surveillance and self-discipline. Using this conception, power is exercised by a gaze; it is

> an inspecting gaze, a gaze which each individual under its weight will end by interiorising to the point that he is his own overseer, each individual thus exercising his surveillance over, and against himself.
>
> (Foucault 1980: 155)

As Caroline Ramazonoglu has noted, feminists have found these ideas useful in revealing the social pressures on women not only to submit to discipline but also to conform to norms by producing their own docile bodies (1993: 22).[2] Many other contemporary writers have developed a Foucauldian approach in order to demonstrate how the 'psy' professions (psychiatry, psychoanalysis, psychology, etc.) have come to prevail in the regulation of family life in the West.[3]

This book makes use of Foucault in the sense that it seeks to reveal and examine the ways in which lone mothers and non-residential fathers have been constructed in discourses about the issues concerning the post-separation family, lone mothers, non-residential fathers, child support and of mothering and fathering more generally. I am particularly concerned with identifying the subject position that the relevant discourses have constituted for lone mothers as they have received much greater disapprobation than have non-residential fathers. I will also examine how

---

2. For an analysis of how eating disorders arise out of normative feminine practices, see Bordo 1990.

3. See, for example, Collier 1995a; Donzelot 1980; Rose 1989; Walkerdine and Lucey 1989.

that subject position is discursively located in power relations as compared with other categories – for example the two-parent household and the non-residential father and also in respect of the general category of maternity.

I will demonstrate that the lone mother headed household is constructed as lacking in comparison with its two-parent counterpart. More specifically, I will show that in cases where the lone mother is represented as wilfully rejecting the traditional family form or as failing to subscribe to legally or socially acceptable behavioural norms, she will at the same time be placed outside the boundaries of appropriate standards of maternal behaviour. I am also concerned to show how mothers live, make sense of and negotiate within and through the network of discursive power relations. The final chapter is dedicated to an analysis of data gathered from a series of interviews with lone mothers where participants tell the stories of their lives as lone mothers.

In order to develop the analysis, I rely upon Foucault's notion of 'apparatus'. In 'The Confession of the Flesh' (1980: 194), he describes the 'apparatus of sexuality' as

> a thoroughly heterogeneous ensemble consisting of discourses,
> institutions, architectural forms, regulatory decisions, laws,
> administrative measures, scientific statements, philosophical,
> moral and philanthropic propositions – in short, the said as
> much as the unsaid.

This book is therefore concerned with examining the system of relations that might be established between the heterogeneous elements that constitute the post-separation family, the specific problem of child support and 'the family', fatherhood and lone motherhood more generally. The elements that feature most highly in this project are political discourse, legal discourse, the discourses of the academy and the popular discourses of the media, most notably press discourses.

I argue that the good mother is constructed and defined through a discourse of her children's needs. The discourses about child support specifically and families more generally have identified the child's need for a father. The mother's caring role is articulated in terms of her meeting the needs of her children. When the lone mother fails to ensure that the child's need for a father is furnished, she is placed outside the realm of good mothering. I will attend to this issue in Chapters 2 and 3. While the mother has needs and desires of her own, these are not explicitly attended to in the discourses that construct her maternal role. I will discuss this point at greater length in Chapter 5.

For now, I wish to highlight that even though constructions by discourse of the perfect mother exist, they can and are capable of being challenged by competing feminist constructions of the different ways in which women can be as mothers. Thus, the construction of the perfect mother can be contested; women can refuse to yield to the regime that attempts to ensure that her child receives financial support from her biological father. However, the site of contestation over the construction of what it is to be this perfect mother is not restricted to feminist concerns. Women may well contest the idea of the perfect mother without wearing the mantle of feminism. To use Janet Ransom's words (1993: 135):

> the social and historical constitution of the subject is not a limit on women's agency but the precondition for women taking action. It is because, and not in spite of, our embeddedness in discursive practices that political action is possible.

Ransom emphasizes the point that Foucault makes about the productive capacity of discourse. In 'Truth and Power', Foucault argues that discourse makes possible a whole range of interventions that have traditionally been seen as repressive. He argues against this that discourse has produced the human subject, and the case he cites here is the sexualized infant (Foucault 1980: 120). It is clear then that although the subject exists as an invention of socially and historically constructed discourses, they also exist as a thinking and emotional person capable of understanding that she is both the source and site of contesting discourses. In other words, she is both constituted and constitutive, and she is constitutive because she is constituted. In this way, the concept of subjectivity becomes central to the feminist research project for it is crucial that women are not merely regarded as a form of cultural hologram waiting to be filled in by discourses. The concept of subjectivity will be discussed further shortly, and suggestions for how it might be incorporated into the feminist research project will also be made here. For now, I wish to focus my attention on two of the main charges made against Foucault: that his work does not succeed in locating any domination in power relations; and it does not account for a form of resistance that is useful to the feminist project.

A feminist critique of Foucault

Nancy Hartsock provides an eloquent and pithy critique against adopting Foucault's analysis of power (1990: 157–75). She accepts that Foucault succeeds in stressing the systemic nature of power and its proliferation in a wide range of social relations. At the same time, however, by emphasizing the heterogeneity and the specificity of particular situations, he loses track of social structures such as the gendered dimensions of female subordination (*ibid.*: 168). Foucault is charged with advocating an individualistic approach to the study of power that focuses on how certain individuals experience and exercise power. Individuals are considered to be constantly circulating among the 'threads of power'. They are in Foucault's words 'always in the position of simultaneously undergoing and exercising this power' (1980: 98).

Individuals are not to be viewed as mere atoms that power is wielded against. Rather, Foucault argues that that certain discourses and bodies are constituted as individuals is an effect of power. In this way, power is not to be regarded as either a single individual dominating another or as one group or class dominating others (*ibid.*). Hartsock notes that on this analysis Foucault has made it difficult to locate domination, including that which is crucial to the feminist project, locating women's subordination in gender relations. She maintains that on the one hand he claims that individuals are constituted by power relations, but on the other hand he argues against the idea that they are constituted by relations such as the domination of one group over another. Thus, his account accommodates only 'abstract individuals, not women, men, or workers' (1990: 169).

She develops this argument further using Foucault's proposition that the nineteenth-century family should be understood as a 'network of pleasures and powers linked together at multiple points' (Foucault 1981: 48). Hartsock makes the claim that the image of the net fails to take into account the important power differentials within the family. She argues further that rather than merely *allowing* for the ignoring of power relations, ironically the image *facilitates* the ignoring of power relations while he is claiming to be elucidating them (Hartsock 1990: 169). According to Hartsock, domination does not figure in this aspect of his work; rather, the image of a network in which we are all participants carries with it 'implications of equality and agency rather than the systematic domination of the many by the few' (*ibid.*). She also posits that the suggestions of equality and agency present in his work have the potential to lead to 'blaming the victim', for if we all participate equally in the network then can it not be said that we are responsible for our own situations? In other words, Hartsock is arguing that the concept of human agency is dissolved and replaced by a passive conception that we are all succumbing to the normalizing tendencies of regimes of discourse.

Notwithstanding Hartsock's critique, I would argue that Foucault's work remains politically relevant to women and feminism for the following reasons. Because of his approach to historical and theoretical method, which stresses the cultural and historical specificity of constructions of sexuality, deviance, madness and criminality, he provides feminism with a variety of strategic possibilities for small-scale analyses. Moreover, his work analyses the manner in which purported objective truths, for example those of the new academic disciplines and sciences, are linked, along with the knowledge they produce, to specific interests. In *History of Sexuality*, vol. 1, he points out that the construction of sexuality as an important issue in the nineteenth century served the interests of the European industrial bourgeoisie and of the developing scientific and medical domains. According to this thesis, sexuality was constructed and employed in order to define what was distinctive and superior about the bourgeoisie in comparison with the degenerate nobility and the depraved lower classes (Foucault 1981: 123–4). Thus, the construction of sexuality in the nineteenth century was crucial in distinguishing and defining the bourgeoisie from other classes. Moreover, the material historical conditions of the time gave rise to the bourgeoisie's employment of its own construction of 'pure' sexuality in order to control people as populations (see further, Bailey 1993: 113–14).

The conclusion may therefore be drawn that in the nineteenth century the construction of sexuality served the interests of the bourgeoisie. It would be inaccurate to say that Foucault is claiming that the bourgeoisie 'held' power, but I would argue that it is reasonable to say that they held an 'interest' in constructing sexuality in a particular way. Additionally, as I go on to show, his work is useful for the feminist project in that it has the capacity to reveal and reclaim the subjugated knowledge of those who have been disqualified. I do not seek, however, to extricate Foucault from Hartsock's and others' charge that his work fails to consider the aspect of gender domination in his work, for I would agree with them that it does. Nevertheless, his work does have particular resonance for feminism.

The question must then be asked as to where all this leaves us in relation to the critique of Foucault posited by Hartsock. Here I will analyse her main points. First, she maintains that while Foucault has noted the systemic nature of power relations he has failed to address (by focusing upon how individuals experience and exercise power at a specific and localized level) the gendered dimensions of female subordination. Hartsock maintains that feminist theory needs to employ broad-based categories such as gender in order to avoid accepting an ontology of abstract individualism. I concur with Hartsock that gender is a category of analysis that remains crucial to the understanding of female subordination.

I maintain against Hartsock that Foucault offers a theoretical basis for avoiding the construction of a theory that generalizes from the experiences of a particular perspective, i.e. that category of women that is white, middle-class and Western, as if their experience defined gender. As Linda Nicholson has observed (1990: 5–6), feminists have frequently employed categories that have tended towards essentialism:

> many feminist theories of the late 1960s to the mid-1980s have been susceptible to the same kinds of criticisms as postmodernists make against philosophy. This point is evident in the attempts by many feminist theorists to locate 'the cause' of women's oppression. Such attempts have ranged from Shulamith Firestone's very early appeal to biological differences between women and men, to the postulation by many influential feminist anthropologists in the 1970s of a cross-cultural domestic/public separation, to later appeals in the late 1970s and early 1980s to women's labor, to women's sexuality, and to women's primary responsibility for child bearing. In all of these cases, aspects of modern Western culture were postulated as present in all or most of human history.

Nicholson elucidates how some feminist writings sought to render as essential the characteristics that were often devalued in Western culture. The work of Mary Daly is exemplary here. Daly held that women must assume and enjoy their essential female nature in order to overcome patriarchy. Moreover, she argued for a concomitant re-evaluation of these characteristics. She posited that femininity is constructed by patriarchy and that as such women should reject everything that the label 'femininity' connotes such as nurturance, compassion and gentleness. For her, femininity is a man-made construct that has nothing to do with femaleness (Daly 1978: 68). For a woman to discover her true and natural self, she has to reject the false identity that patriarchy has constructed for her to get to the essential woman underneath.

Although her work was useful for pointing out how those characteristics that are traditionally described as 'female' are often devalued, she sought to impose an alternative identity on women that many felt alienated from. In effect, while some women may have felt that they were being offered new ways of perceiving their lives and new possibilities for acting out those lives, others who did not experience the postulated 'essential' female nature were marginalized. Daly's theory is problematic precisely because of its essentialism. It projects onto all women and men qualities that develop under socially and historically specific conditions.

As Fraser and Nicholson point out, essentialist theory is also often monocausal in that it regards one set of characteristics as sufficient to explain women's oppression across cultures (1990: 28). Fraser and Nicholson conclude that 'quasi-metanarratives' that focus upon a supposed cross-cultural activity such as mothering foreclose any investigation of its historical origins and fail as a result to account for the historical specificity of particular categories such as the modern, nuclear family. Moreover, they also claim that:

> categories like sexuality, mothering, reproduction, and sex-affective production group together phenomena which are not necessarily conjoined in all societies while separating off from one another phenomena which are not necessarily separated.   (*ibid.*: 31)

The dangers with developing a theory that seeks to have universal application are all too apparent. The theorist may well project the dominant culturally and historically specific conjunctions/separations of her own society onto other societies, thus distorting important elements of both. In other words, the theorist runs the risk of assuming the universality of general categories without getting to grips with the way that the categories have come to develop in our own culture.

The point I am labouring here is that Foucault reminds us to avoid making generalizations that transcend historical and cultural boundaries. I am arguing that feminists should situate discussion of general categories in a social and historical context rather than making assumptions based upon preconceptions that history is the history of men's oppression of women. Against Hartsock, I would argue that Foucault's theoretical framework offers feminism the potential for identifying those types of theorizing that are hostile to essentialism, thus providing the opportunity to avoid false generalizations that may have no bearing on the lives of women in all their diversity. Additionally, whenever general categories are employed, adopting a Foucauldian analysis will mean that they are firmly situated within a specific cultural and historical context. Rather than employ ahistorical categories such as mothering and biology, theoretical and practical work should concentrate on inflecting the categories to reflect the transient, culturally specific nature of these classifications. So, for example, rather than focusing upon broad categories such as mothering, feminists should look to understand how aspects of mothering are impacted upon by their social and historical context. This makes it possible to understand better the way that women are oppressed 'as women' (Ransom 1993: 132). As Phelan points out:

Foucault's work should lead us to suspect that these various sites of oppression are indeed various, that we must examine them in their particularity, as operations that may oppose and challenge one another even as they tend towards a common end for women.

(1990: 2)

Phelan's account of Foucault's conception of power is clearly sympathetic. She argues in contrast to Hartsock that his conception of power has utility for the feminist project. She advocates a mode of analysis that focuses upon specific sites of oppression. At the same time, it should be remembered that sites of oppression are various and the operations of power are sometimes contradictory and opposed to each other. They are thus unstable and ephemeral even when there is a drive towards a common end for women. Phelan's sense of the utility of Foucault for feminism permits a conception of power that can account for the complexities of its various operations. As such, it forestalls an over-simplified version of the operation of power as being straightforwardly out there and affecting all women in exactly the same way.

To relate this to the project in hand, preconceptions of what motherhood entails for women should be supplanted by a new way of looking at motherhood based upon how legal and social changes have come to affect the dominant conceptions of motherhood as a social practice. While the dominant conceptions of motherhood may still reflect the idea that mothers should assume the majority of the caring responsibility for their children, this conception has been usurped by social and economic changes that place women, both married and unmarried, more frequently outside the home. The retention of social and legal discourses that seek to posit the ideology of the mother as full-time carer have the effect of locating the working mother within a complex set of contradictory messages.

On the one hand, legal and social discourses continue to reflect the idea of the traditional nuclear family in which the mother cares and the man provides. On the other hand, social and economic factors such as high male unemployment, increased access to paid work for women and the state's increasing emphasis upon the notion that families should be self-reliant all serve to encourage women's participation in work outside the home. When the mother in question is a lone mother who relies upon state benefits for support, the dominant privileging of the stay-at-home mother serves to heighten her awareness of these contradictions. Moreover, she may well experience feelings of frustration due to the proliferation of these conflicting and inconsistent formations. Some of the women who participated in this project spoke of strong feelings of 'damned if you do, damned if you don't'. Moreover, when explicitly asked to comment upon the way in which lone mothers are portrayed by discourses generated by a number of sources, particularly the media and government officials, they voiced their grievances about the way they had been constructed by these discourses.

This leads to a consideration of the second of Hartsock's criticisms of Foucault. She claims that he fails to provide any useful concept of human agency and that he tends towards the idea of the individual participating in her own domination rather than developing a theory of resistance that is politically useful for women. I believe that although Foucault may not be able to withstand the charge that he did not specifically address the way that women experience the effects of the powers of discourse differently to men, his analysis of power does allow for the investigation of how discourses give rise to forms of resistance. He writes:

> Discourses are not once and for all subservient to power or raised up against it, any more than silences are. We must make allowance for the complex and unstable process whereby discourse can be both an instrument and an effect of power, but also a hindrance; a stumbling block, a point of resistance and a starting point for an opening strategy.
>
> (Foucault 1981: 100–1)

Here, Foucault is once again rendering explicit his view that discourse is generative and productive. Once it is understood how discourses manufacture disciplinary power the opportunity arises for analysing the way that discourses spawn forms of subjectivity. In this way, power relations are not stagnant; rather, women are able to develop alternative subjectivities, subjectivities that refuse the prevailing dominant constructions that discourses have created for them. Rather than undercutting the notion of agency and resistance as is alleged by Hartsock, Foucault's theory centralizes the notion of subjectivity by conceiving it as both the site and source of discourses. Thus, although the subject is socially and legally constructed, at the same time she exists as a 'thinking, feeling and social subject and agent, capable of resistance and innovations produced out of the clash between contradictory subject positions and practices' (Weedon 1987: 125).

In this book, I identify several sources of regulatory apparatus and techniques of power that construct the subjectivities of lone mothers and non-residential fathers. I have elected to focus particularly upon the apparatuses of the state, the law and the media. In addition, I have included the stories of those women who have been marginalized in contemporary discourses about families, lone mothers, father absence and child support. I aim to show how the subjectivities of women and men are constructed in terms of their relevance and significance for 'the family' both within and without the law in debates about the 'problem' of providing for children in the event of a relationship breakdown. This should not be taken to mean that there is either one constructed singular, unified and static concept of the family or one female/male subjectivity that is constituted and reproduced with consistency throughout legal and social discourses about women, men, mothers, fathers and families. The subjectivities of mothers and fathers are ascribed with different meanings according to their various historical, social and legal contexts. For example, American writer Susan Boyd has noted an 'extraordinarily positive judicial approbation' of the lone mother, who is constructed as 'supermom' if she excels at her career at the same time as being a devoted mother. Her argument is that the ideology of motherhood takes new forms as the discourse structures concerning parenting and family form shift (1996: 511).

One of the most prominent ideas in contemporary discourses of lone motherhood supports the notion that the way out of poverty for lone mothers is to work in the labour market. In Chapter 5, I discuss the case of Heidi Colwell, who attempted to support herself through employment outside the home but failed to demonstrate 'supermom' status because of her failure to provide at the same time the legally defined acceptable level of care for her daughter. While it may not be appropriate to say that there is one single construction of the mother in legal and social discourses, it is possible to identify a valorized subject position against which other subject positions will be compared, contrasted and measured. If lone mothers fall short of the idealized subjectivity, then a lower status is ascribed to them than is accorded to the socially or legally privileged. Just as there is no one unified subject in legal and social discourses, the regulatory practices and apparatuses that construct subjectivities are diverse and contradictory. In Rose's opinion:

> spaces, activities and relations which are within the scope of regulation for one purpose are outside it for another. Unities and coherences must be analysed in terms of outcomes rather than origins or intentions. Rather than conferring a false unity upon the diversity of legal regulation, critical analysis should treat this diversity as both a clue to the intelligibility of the law and, perhaps, as the key to a political strategy in relation to law. (1987: 67)

The implication of the above for the analysis of the post-separation family, lone motherhood and fatherhood is that there is not necessarily any consistency of impact and effect of the regulatory powers of the state, the law or the media. It would be naive to suggest that there is a consistency of application in a single field of regulatory practices such as within the law, let alone that there is any coherence across the various fields of discourse. In other words, the relationships between the discourses or regulatory practices of the state, the law, the family and the media can be characterized as inconsistent, fractured and having unequal application.

Inherent contradictions exist both *within* the various regulatory practices and *between* them. It is clear from Rose that the diversity of regulation should be encountered and tackled head on for the sake of understanding its potency and for the sake of political expediency. It is therefore not possible to say that there is a consolidated policy about lone motherhood that derives from a variety of institutions across the law, the state and the media. Rather, the constitution of the lone mother occurs in a kaleidoscopic network of legal, academic, media and state discourses on motherhood and 'the family'.

This project is motivated by a desire to examine the diversity of the relations between the subject – the lone mother – the non-residential father and the various apparatuses that constitute them. By so doing, I want to reveal something about what it means to be a lone mother in contemporary society. The emphasis is upon discovering the *sociality* of the lone mother. My project is not merely concerned with how lone mothers are constituted in and by the complex network of power relations and where they are located within it. My aim is also to consider the ways in which they themselves negotiate in and through that network. Given the centrality of the concept of subjectivity to the book, along with the recognition that certain discourses have authority over others, it becomes crucial to include the voices of those who have been silenced or neglected in discourses about lone motherhood, the voices of the lone mothers themselves. I argue against Hartsock that Foucauldian analysis remains useful to the feminist project in that it provides insight into the ways in which power is exercised through the meanings that are ascribed by the apparatuses of regulation and gives rise to a potential for the inclusion of previously subjugated knowledge. At this juncture, I will discuss the notions of subjectivity and experience and outline the manner in which they have relevance and application for feminist practice generally and for this project in particular.

Returning the Subject to the subject of women's poverty

> Within women's politics there are some aspects that go beyond
> economism, such as the strengthening of subjectivity, the
> consideration given to qualitative differences, the recognition
> of the significance of the symbolic. Aside from all that, there is
> female experience.
>
> (Muraro 1993: 98)

Luisa Muraro does not continue to develop what she means
when she talks of the political expediency of female experience and the
strengthening of subjectivity. However, Elspeth Probyn eloquently articulates the importance of the concept of experience:

> experience can be made to work in two registers: at an ontological
> level, the concept of experience posits a separate realm of existence
> – it testifies to the gendered, sexual and racial facticity of being
> in the social; it can be called an immediate experiential self. At an
> epistemological level, the self is revealed in its conditions of
> possibility; here experience is recognized as more obviously discursive
> and can be used to overtly politicize the ontological.   (1993: 16)

Probyn's two-strand concept of experience is useful because at the
level of ontology or immediate experience it enables account to be taken
of the differences between women based upon their separateness from each
other and upon the facts of their social positioning in relation to gender,
race, ethnicity and sexuality. She refers to this level as the 'immediate experiential self'. At the epistemological level, experience is regarded as more
obviously relevant to discourse and is utilized to politicize the ontological. In other words, Probyn acknowledges the socially constructed nature
of the first level of being, but she argues that the second sense is clearly
more obviously relevant and politically useful for politicizing the first sense.
She maintains that both these levels of experience are necessary conditions for enabling alternative speaking positions within cultural studies.
Her concern with developing the two-strand approach is therefore prag-
matic. The epistemological level operates to locate and problematize the
conditions that permit or limit individuated experience; the ontological
level serves to stress that the epistemological understanding of experience
should not overwhelm and undermine the importance of the ontological level of experience for fear of marginalizing this level. She argues that
by adopting the two-strand approach to experience the cultural critic is

enabled to travel beyond the idea that experience can be reduced to a guarantee of authenticity.

Probyn therefore states that the two levels of experience are essential to creating an understanding of experience that goes beyond an
attempt to posit a 'truth' or authenticity about an individual towards an
understanding of the historical conditions of speaking in terms of one's
own experiences. As Young has indicated: 'the discourse we use when
we describe our experience is no more direct and unmediated than any
other discourse; it is only discourse in a different mode' (1990: 12). Both
Probyn and Young are seeking to get away from the idea of the authentic
and true self, preferring instead to promote the use of experience as a
heuristic tool for unearthing the social and historical conditions involved
in the articulation of the self. Both writers are concerned with the pragmatics of experience. Description of experience allows for the naming
of forms and meanings of oppression. The subject's description of their
social world brings to language the feelings of harm and suffering that
are encountered as a result of oppressive regimes. Moreover, through the
experiential description of social life, the opportunity arises for the possibility of resistance as 'experience names a moment of creative agency in
social processes, which cannot be finally totalized or categorized by the
dominant oppressive structures' (ibid.: 14). As such, by identifying and naming different kinds of oppression and by articulating the experiences of
oppression, the creative agency of the oppressed allows for resistance and
a rejection of the oppressive regimes. In other words, with regard to the
women who participated in this project, the identification and naming of
oppressive apparatuses of power helps them to form alternative conceptions that constitute a resistance to that oppression and the creation of
alternative conceptions. As an enunciative position within the law and the
social, experience is useful for articulating the social differentiations of
gender, sexuality, class, ethnicity and race.

As Young points out, it is important that a 'renewed theorization of
experience sets out the conditions of possibility for the construction of a
new, empowered speaking position within cultural theory' (ibid.: 30). The
concept of experience is useful for understanding that subjectivity is constituted by contradictory, shifting discourses and social practices within
which the subject always and inevitably finds herself already implicated.
At the same time, subjects are themselves constitutive and creative; they
react and respond to their constituted selves and act in accordance or dis-
cordance with and from the construction.

My own concern with developing an approach to the study of
women's oppression that incorporates experience also lies in the realm of

pragmatics. My interest is in describing the processes of social life from the point of view of the subject. Rather than use experience as the key notion for her analysis, Chris Weedon prefers to use the term 'subjectivity'. It occurs to me, however, that her notion of subjectivity is extremely similar to Probyn's concept of experience. For Weedon, the concept of subjectivity pertains to the conscious and unconscious thoughts, reflections and emotions of the individual, how she views herself in relation to other societal members, institutional forces, and society as a whole, and how she makes sense of, and understands, her position in that society. Subjectivity is not a static concept that once elucidated remains as a signifier of what that woman is for ever. It is not possible to capture subjectivity, put it in a cage and expect it to remain the same, for the action of capture will change the woman's view of her world. As such, subjectivity is always in flux, constantly reconstituting itself, with the individual being both the source and site of conflicting and changing forms of subjectivity (Weedon 1987: 32–3).[4] Weedon's concept of subjectivity contains both senses of Probyn's formulation of the ontological and epistemological aspects of experience. It both appeals to the idea of the immediate experiential self and testifies to the idea that the self is revealed in its conditions of possibility. However, Weedon's concept of subjectivity differs from Probyn's formulation of experience in that it does not make the two levels of experience analytically distinct. Nevertheless, the two concepts are close enough to allow the two terms 'experience' and 'subjectivity' to be used interchangeably for the purposes of this project.

The utility of experience

Having established at least to some extent the significance of experience, it is important to stress its pertinence for feminist research methodology. Feminist academic debates about women in any context initially stemmed from a desire to unearth and challenge structures of male privilege and domination. Feminism operates to counter the fact that women have either been omitted in accounts of the social world or have been incorporated into male ways of knowing, which bear little if any resemblance

---

4. See also Luce Irigaray (1987), who urges women to reclaim their subjectivity by rejecting both the idea and the use of the gender-neutral voice, which she claims is a passive voice that distances the subject from the object and conceals the identity of the speaker from the reader. For her, only when women speak in an active, gendered voice do they avoid the false security and inauthenticity of the passive voice.

to how women actually perceive themselves in relation to the rest of the world. As demonstrated earlier, discourses not only constitute us, they also have the capacity to ensure the subject's self-regulation. The phenomenon of internalized oppression is only possible because of the effects these discourses have (Spelman and Lugones 1993). The process of interaction, of speaking, hearing, listening and response, should be one in which the participant can recognize herself as a major player in the writing of the story about her life. The process should provide a means of mutual discovery for both the researcher and the researched.

But the question is then raised as to whose are the voices that should be heard?[5] In debates on the subject of familial poverty, it is crucial to give voice to those women who directly experience poverty and all its concomitants, including mechanisms such as the Child Support Act that are allegedly set up as a means by which women's economic position may be ameliorated. The measure of poverty and ways of experiencing it are multifarious and diverse, depending upon how the individual constructs the issue of poverty and how she sees herself in relation to it. In order to illustrate my point, two cameos are juxtaposed.

A lone mother earning an amount of money over and above state benefit level may regard herself as poor in comparison with her ex-partner if he earns a good deal more in self-employment. Additionally, because the Child Support Agency has persistently found cases involving the self-employed 'difficult', she is unable to secure maintenance from him. See, for example, the report in *The Guardian* (28 January 1994), where a lone parent suffered a reduction in her maintenance award from £300 per month to £57.43 a week allegedly because of the agency's inability to deal with cases where the man is self-employed. The failure to deal with the self-employed is currently under review by the present Labour government, which intends to recover debts through various means such as deducting money from bank accounts and using bailiffs to recover assets (HMSO 1998: 30).

In my second scenario, a woman who relies solely upon income support for her own and her children's upkeep and has an ex-partner who

---

5. A number of practical implications are raised by this question, such as how do we ensure that a range of voices are heard? In order to ensure that I drew in a cross-section of women into my research I placed an advertisement calling for participants in *The Guardian*. I ask *Woman's Own* and *Woman* magazines to run the ad, but they both refused. I ran an ad in *Shebang*, a free lesbian publication, and I also ran an ad in the local paper, the *Lancaster Guardian*.

is himself dependent upon state benefits will construct and experience poverty in a different way. Both women will believe themselves to be poor even though their location in the network of power relations is at variance. This can be explained by the way that they make sense of their lives in relation to their position within the network, drawing upon comparisons made between themselves and others who may or may not be better off.

It is my contention that experience is crucial to the debate on familial poverty because inclusion of it in any feminist discourse serves to fill the lacunae that 'talking principles' creates, gaps where differences of race, class, ethnicity, sexual alliance and religion should reside. I will return to this point in the next section. To ensure that these gaps are filled, feminist research requires more than developing theories about the reasons for women's oppression. Feminist research also involves more than discovering how discourses are imbued with and generative of power. Researching women's lives should also incorporate fundamental, practical activity. In the words of Sheila Rowbotham: 'Searching for the lost female subject involves us in re-searching, in its literal sense. We have to return to the world and begin to observe, listen and record' (cited in Graham 1984: 122).

Interviewing is a qualitative information-gathering technique that has been used by a great number of feminist researchers in past years and to the present day, with semi-structured, unstructured, in-depth and open-ended being the predominant forms. Traditionally, the technique was employed within a specific academic context that stressed the role of social scientists as collectors and analysts of objectively verifiable data. Women participating in research were effectively treated merely as data providers (Oakley 1985: xi). Oakley argues for a renunciation of objectification on the grounds that it 'undermines the very importance of subjectivity in the mapping of social experience' (*ibid.*). She clearly castigates the paradigms of traditional interviewing practices, including the idea that the interview is a one-way process with the interviewer eliciting and receiving information but imparting none. She suggests that the open-ended interview can and should encourage interplay between interviewer and interviewee, in an attempt to avoid both the creation of a hierarchical relationship and the objectification of women participants (Oakley 1981).[6] Graham has also stated that the interview is the principal means by which feminist researchers have sought to achieve the active involvement of women in the construction of data about their lives (1984: 114–15).

---

6.   See also Janet Finch (1984), who adopts Oakley's model for these reasons.

Notwithstanding that feminists have sought to incorporate the active participation of women into the construction of data about their own lives by means of interviewing, the technique is not without its ethical and methodological problems. The researcher starts with the presumption that there is something 'out there' that will be useful as a means of revealing the ways in which women experience oppression. Moreover, the technique requires that women be able to identify and articulate what form the oppression takes. The researcher is trying to solicit information with a particular project or aim in mind. In my case, I wanted to unearth the extent (if any) to which women were affected by the representations made of them in political, legal and social discourses. In order to do this, I needed to formulate an agenda for study. By setting out this agenda and by attempting to draw together a string of 'subjugated knowledges', am I not merely replicating the problematic of the power/knowledge strategies identified by Foucault, obtaining the 'confession in order to found new knowledge?'. Foucault argues that:

> One does not confess without the presence (or virtual presence) of a partner who is not simply the interlocutor but the authority who requires the confession, prescribes and appreciates it, and intervenes in order to judge, punish, forgive, console and reconcile; a ritual in which the truth is corroborated by the obstacles and resistancies it has to surmount in order to be formulated.   (Foucault 1981: 61–2)

As the designer and instigator of the research project, I am responsible for setting the agenda for study. There is a potential danger of the interviewer assuming the position of authoritative interrogator with the power to listen, appreciate, intervene and adjudicate accordingly. But as Vikki Bell points out, the power relationship that exists between the researcher and the participant (in her case the incest survivor) is not the same as the one that exists between 'analyst and analysand, nor that between accused and court'. Feminist researchers attempt to minimize the participant's discomfort. They will respect her desire for privacy in matters about which she does not want to or feels unable to talk, in contrast to the determination to have the participant reveal all the minutiae of her personal life (Bell 1993: 103–4). The aim of the interview is not to discover an essential 'truth' about the participant in order to judge and punish, as is the case with the Foucauldian concept of confession. Rather, the interview is used in order to learn about how the participants understand and negotiate their lives in and through the network of discursive power relations. As Bell rightly says, the feminist researcher is not the authority or the adjudicator in the same way that legal agents can be.

It is my suggestion that the feminist researcher should try to come as close as is possible to positioning herself as the interlocutor. What I mean by this is that feminist researchers should adopt the model of interview put forward by Ann Oakley in an attempt to avoid the creation of a hierarchical relationship and the objectification of women participants (1981). The interviewer or interlocutor should strive towards a dialogue based upon trust, mutuality and reciprocity. The researcher should seek to secure a relationship based upon trust, and trust can only be established if the researcher divulges her own motivations for and interest in the project in hand. Many feminist researchers have remarked that participants like to place the interviewer as women with whom they can share experiences (see, for example, Finch 1984 and Oakley 1981). Once projects are constructed in this manner, researchers can strive to establish what has become known as 'true dialogue' rather than 'interrogation', with participants becoming 'co-researchers' (Bristow and Esper 1988: 67–81).

The establishment of a trusting relationship can be problematic for the participants. Feminist researchers have noted that the effectiveness of research techniques based upon the trusting relationship can result in the participant being rendered vulnerable. The technique can be used to solicit a range of information (some of it very personal), which can be used against the women who impart it freely and willingly (Finch 1984: 82). The feminist researcher owes the participant a responsibility to consider at length how the work might be received and interpreted once it enters the public domain. Of course, guarantees that research will not be used against the women who participate in it cannot be issued. But researchers do owe a duty to the women who have put their trust in them to at least attempt to consider the possibility, for aside from the individual responsibility that the researcher owes to the participant, there is also a collective interest at stake. There is always the very real danger that research may be used against the interests of lone mothers as a group, a possibility that is repugnant to the researcher with feminist commitments (*ibid.*: 83).

Another problem that may arise in feminist research that seeks to stress the importance of incorporating subjectivity is that there is always the possibility that the interviewee will be misunderstood and misrepresented or even rejected in the research process. Questions are thus raised as to the nature of the relationship between the participant's own account of her experiences and the researcher's account of them. The project of understanding and empathizing with another woman is perhaps aided by a sharing of cultural beliefs and patterns. Where women do not share cultural beliefs and backgrounds, discussion must render these cultural differences explicit and recognize that the debate is one that takes place between 'insiders' and 'outsiders' (Spelman and Lugones 1993: 384). However, the researcher is inevitably outside, by the very nature of her role as researcher, despite any possible cultural similarities that she may share with the participant. For example, I am a lone parent from a working-class background, and I have experienced life on income support. I recognize that these facets of my life influence my choice of research topic. But despite the similarities of background I may share or have shared with potential participants, my present position as researcher in an educational institution serves to set me apart from the participant and outside direct experience of the realm of study. The participant is the 'insider'; she has offered to share her experiences inside the field of study with me, the 'outsider'. As the outsider, I am ethically obliged to make clear my intentions for the research, and my motivations for instigating it. In other words, I am declaring my own political partiality with regard to the project. Only when I have divulged this kind of information to my participants can I hope to achieve open and honest dialogue. It is also crucial that the insider/outsider dichotomy be borne in mind when writing up the project, acknowledging when the participant is speaking in her own voice as insider and when it is my voice as researcher and outsider interpreting the insider's own account of herself.[7]

Researchers Bombyk *et al.* note that the concern for mutuality and reciprocity causes problems in the interview situation. Interviewees can be intimidated by the interviewer's self-disclosure, and this may result in a self-censoring process. A participant in their research project remarked how she began to stereotype the interviewer as a result of the interviewer's personal sharing. The participant began to answer questions based upon the perceptions she had made about the interviewer, what she believed she would want to hear, and not what she, as interviewee, really thought. In this case, the problem was made explicit by the interviewee, and once she had notified the interviewer of the problem she felt a greater sense of control over the interview situation; after some time and further discussion, she was in fact keen to know more about the interviewer. The interviewer also learned an invaluable lesson as a result of the exposure of the problem, namely that timing is crucial to the value of self-disclosure

---

7. A number of practical considerations could be raised here, such as how to document the accounts imparted by participants. I have elected in this piece to restrict my account to the theoretical questions raised by doing feminist research.

(Bombyk *et al.* 1985). I would add that another benefit that accrues from the obvious openness of the approach is that it creates the kind of environment that provides the opportunity for such an honest interchange.

Probyn's concept of experience also has implications for the feminist researcher in the interview situation. She maintains that by adopting her two-strand approach to experience critical enterprise moves beyond the construction of experience as an object that is to be studied in a detached and impersonal manner (1993: 23). As a result of accepting this understanding of experience, the researcher is allowed to position herself within the project. She is reminded that her experience is indeed an important part of the overall critical project, and it serves to negotiate between the ontological pull to define experience as primary and transcendental and an epistemological tendency to privilege structural determinants of knowledge (*ibid.*: 26). Probyn's definition of experience is useful because it reminds us that all human experience is mediated by discourse. In this way, the researcher is not attempting to establish a truth about a woman/ women but rather her task lies with investigating the power/knowledge relations within which the participant is defined and negotiates her life. This is also true in relation to the discussion that takes place between the participant and the researcher. Interviewing has the asset of offering the researcher access to people's thoughts and ideas based upon their own lived experiences. It is an asset that is crucial to the study of women, for it can take into account the diversity of women's voices and place them on an agenda for learning about women's lives. Furthermore, it can serve as an antidote to centuries of either ignoring women's perspective altogether or having only men or white, middle-class women speak for them (Reinharz 1992: 19). But the benefits that can accrue are not only for the feminist researcher being satisfied that she has produced work of a fine quality. The women who volunteer to participate in the research have the opportunity to talk about their lives, give their own accounts and hopefully make sense of them in relation to the context of the discussion. In this way, participation in research can be a means of empowerment for women, for in talking about one's life one is actively participating in it, helping to shape it and understand the structural factors that affect it. There may also be a realization of the need for social and political change and a desire to become involved with campaigns for reform. I received letters from women who expressed an interest in participating in my research, who were keen to know what direction my work would take and whether or not it would be sympathetic to the plight of lone mothers. I felt that their concern might stem from the then Conservative government and media attacks on lone parents. In this section, I have stated my case for the importance of the inclusion of experience in the study of women's poverty. I believe that the relevance of the ideas discussed herein is not confined to this one research area, for the project of incorporation of experience has a potential utility for fields of research that have a pertinence to the practical realities of women's lives.

Talking principles/evacuating the Subject

During the early days of my thinking about this research project, I attended a conference on the subject of women's poverty. This conference experience was to influence and inform the methodological concerns of this book. The conference programme included a number of papers on the issue of lone mothers, poverty and child support, which tied in closely with my own research interests. In attendance were legal practitioners, other academics of both genders, female activists with the interest of campaigning against the Child Support Act, and others interested in campaigning against injustice to women at a more general level. There were a number of presentations by female academics, female representatives from two well-known national support groups, and a female delegate from the Child Support Agency, the administrative body responsible for implementing the Act.

The first speaker (who was a representative from one of the women's support groups) had delivered her paper, which included an acclamation of the worth of the basic principle underpinning the first Child Support Act, which was at that time and remains (despite the reforms of 1995 and recent Labour government reform proposals) that natural parents should be held responsible for the financial maintenance of all their biological children after the relationship between the parents has broken down. Where the estranged partner, usually a man, is a high earner and the parent with care is dependent upon income support or earnings in employment, the woman's income can be substantially increased to redress previous imbalances between the parents' incomes. At the time of the Child Support Act's implementation, this was to become known as the 'balance principle'. After the initial speaker's address, members of the audience were invited to put their questions. The first response did not come in the form of a question but instead was an observation pertaining to the speaker's comment that the principle underpinning the Child Support Act was a good one. It was observed that the Child Support Act did nothing to ameliorate the lives of those women in receipt of state benefits, for any maintenance due to them would be deducted pound for pound from their benefit payment.[8] It was also noted that rather than improving the lives of those lone parents on state benefit, women's safety was frequently jeopardized due to the aggressive reaction of their estranged partners when contacted by the Child Support Agency.[9]

The initial speaker reacted to the respondent's comments in a manner that both surprised and upset me. She stated that she knew the audience member's opinion well already because she had followed the speaker from conference to conference making the same points. The official speaker appeared ill at ease and irritable. After she had completed her address, the atmosphere in the meeting was awkward and uncomfortable. The chairperson attempted to stave off further conflict from then on by restricting the respondent to asking questions rather than making comments. It later became apparent that the respondent was a member of the Campaign Against the Child Support Act, an activist.

The conflict between the two delegates, which set the tone for the rest of the conference (marginalizing the activist's experiences as a lone parent in poverty and putting other speakers on guard) consolidated my belief in the importance of incorporating lived experience into feminist research. The marginalization of the lone mother in the process of theorizing about women's poverty highlights the potential for tension and conflict between the two strands of experience as outlined by Probyn. Poverty is experienced at the level of the everyday and not at the level of the formulated abstract principle. It is vital that not just the voices of those women who speak with the authority of the academic podium be heard. If this were to be the case, then there is a very real danger of widening the apparently existing gulf between those who theorize and those who actively campaign for reform in particular areas that directly affect their lives. It is crucial that women who speak from a more powerful position show respect for and acknowledgement of the experiences of those women who are in a more vulnerable position due to their socio-economic status.

---

8.   The Labour government has since proposed that lone mothers in receipt of state benefit should keep £10 before deductions are made.

9.   These observations were based upon my respondent's personal experiences. Violent responses, however, were not necessarily confined to those women who stand to gain nothing financially from the pursuit of maintenance. I had at the time of writing received letters from women expressing an interest in participating in my research, whose husbands were high wage earners and as such stood to gain financially as a result. They have also spoken of violence perpetrated against them by their angry ex-partners.

At this point, I want to return to the 'balance principle', which refers to the way the Act attempts to redress the previous imbalance between the lone parent's (90 per cent of whom are women) income and the estranged partner's income (concomitantly, usually men) (National Council for One Parent Families 1993 [NCOPF]). On a previous occasion, the speaker had expressed continuing and public concern that 'gross inequalities' between first and second families should be ironed out. In *The Guardian* (6 September 1994), she was quoted as saying: 'We need a formula that establishes a principle of equity between families.'

The balance principle is also evident in the then Conservative government's original White Paper, where it is stated that: 'A fair and reasonable balance has to be struck between the interests of the children of a first family and the children of a second' (HMSO 1990: para. 2.1). The Act sets out to achieve this balance by replacing the discretionary system of collecting child maintenance, as enforced by the courts under the Matrimonial and Family Proceedings Act 1984, with a formula designed to achieve certainty and consistency of application. Under the previous system, courts sought to effect wherever possible a clean break between parties to the divorce while also taking into consideration any children's interests according to Section 25 MFPA 1984. In practice, a nominal sum of ongoing child maintenance was often awarded on the basis that parents could not expect to make a clean break from their natural children.

Courts both recognized and acted upon the idea that frequently the financial capability of a standard wage earner did not extend to maintaining two households. In a case preceding the new legislation, the Court of Appeal regarded it as unrealistic to expect a former partner to pay a weekly maintenance order of £30 when he had established a home with a new partner on a wage of £115 per week. The presiding judges held that the courts could not avoid recognizing the availability of state benefits as a potential source of income for the former family, and they substituted the claim for the £30 maintenance award with a nominal order.[10] As noted by Gibson, it would appear that the courts accepted that the wage structure designed for the support of one household limited the amount of maintenance to be paid to the first family if the estranged partner had embarked upon a new relationship carrying fresh financial responsibilities (1994: 208). In enacting the Child Support Act, the then Conservative government sought to alter this trend in favour, it claims, of striking a fairer balance between first and subsequent families.

---

10. Delaney *v.* Delaney [1990] 2 FLR 457.

The question is therefore raised as to what extent the new provisions were effective in redressing the previous imbalance. It soon became clear that in many cases the lone mother stood to benefit nothing in financial terms from non-residential fathers who are in receipt of low incomes or state benefits. The Payday men's network claimed that a non-residential father (assuming he paid £50 per week housing costs and had no other children) would have to earn over £203 per week net in order for his estranged partner with two children to come off income support (1990). Even if the lone mother is successful in coming off benefit, she may find herself in a worse financial position due to the loss of 'passported' benefits, such as free school meals, clothing allowance and council tax reduction. Passported benefits are those that lone mothers are entitled to as a result of their claiming social security benefits.

With over one million men in receipt of unemployment benefit and many more in low-paid jobs, a great number of lone mothers did not have their incomes raised above the rate they received prior to the Act's implementation. The Act forced women to rely upon men they no longer wished to have any contact with. It should be noted, however, that under the old system DSS officers also had powers to enforce child maintenance against non-residential fathers. But past policy recognized that the financial capability of a standard wage earner did not extend to maintaining two households. When it came to deciding between the claims of the former family and the new one, there was an assumption that it was easier to enforce maintenance for the new family.

Under the original rules of the new system, the Act effectively shifted the financial burden away from the state and back to the private sphere, where the ramifications for newly formed second families proved to be severe. In effect, the new legislation frequently created an environment (or intensified an existing situation) in which the former family and newly formed family found themselves pitted against each other. Both families staked their claim for financial support based upon the status of their children, with biological children taking priority. At its outset, the child support formula did not make allowance for the *de facto* responsibilities for step-children. No allowance was incorporated into the income exemptions used in the calculation of assessable income. But there was some recognition in the protected income, set slightly above the level of income support. As a result of vehement criticism from many quarters, this was amended in the Child Support Act 1995 and again in the most recent proposals by the present Labour government. It has been noted that many of the concessions made since the Act's implementation have served to benefit the situation of non-residential fathers and their reconstituted families (for a detailed discussion of these concessions, see Diduck and Kaganas 1999: 396–403).

Given the Conservative government's desire to drive financial responsibility back to the private sphere and away from the state, the financial penalties that were effectively imposed by the state's discriminatory treatment of step-children and biological children proved to be erroneous. The government jeopardized both its own programme to reduce public expenditure and the financial and emotional well-being of step-children. When step-children constituted part of a new family that also contained biological children, they were under the original rules accorded a lower status than biological children for the purposes of the assessment and enforcement of child support. The distinction between biological children and step-children made inroads into the legal concept of 'the child of the family'. This concept reflected the erosion of traditional kinship patterns incidental to increasing divorce and remarriage. Bainham and Cretney have argued that the concept renders the existence of a biological relationship between parties irrelevant (1993: 317–18). It can be argued therefore that the framing of the Child Support Act 1991 forged a huge chasm in a concept that was designed to eradicate such distinctions. The government's first report on the operation of the Child Support Act highlighted one of the main problems arising from the distinction made between these children. The Social Security Committee provided evidence from the National Stepfamily Association, which observed that while children may be assessed as carrying similar financial burdens, the biological parents of the respective children will not necessarily have parity of resources. And in their proffered example of such a case, it is noted how one father was assessed to pay an increased amount of £515 per month in order to support his two biological children, while his two step-children's father had been assessed to pay a sum of £20 per month. The association believed that the stepfamily was suffering as a result (Social Security Committee 1994: para. 80). There are a number of points to be raised here. First, this is the type of situation that fuelled the vehemence of the response towards the Act by many non-residential fathers, who were required to pay a much larger amount of maintenance than they had under the previous system, sometimes having also opted for the clean break settlement. The nature of this response contributed to the changes proposed by the Social Security Committee's first and fifth reports. Second, in situations where the parent with care was in receipt of income support, the Act did appear to be achieving its purported aim of striking a balance between first and subsequent families. But the balance was effectively struck in many instances by taking the second family down to the minimum income level, based upon current Child Support Act rates. Cases reported in the press claimed that non-residential fathers, aggrieved by the manner in which a huge chunk of their wages was being allocated to their former family, would lose their incentive to work. In *The Guardian* (18 May 1994), it was reported that a non-residential father had resigned from his job as a senior local government engineer because 45 per cent of his disposable income of £21,000 per year was to go to his first family. This left 55 per cent for the new family of six. The government could have found itself with an even greater number of families to support if this had become a trend. As a brief aside, the Child Support Act served, in these situations, to alienate many of the government's longstanding supporters, with the phrase 'Thatcher's children' carrying a greatly altered resonance.

However, in a number of cases where the former partner is completely independent of state support, receiving her main income from paid employment, there may be in existence a balance between the two families that takes neither into a position of vulnerability. Here, the parent with care would have to be in a fairly high income bracket to take her above the income support rate. However, the employment market offers women limited availability of well-paid work with suitable conditions. The work may need to be both local and on a part-time basis. Even when such work is available, employers may not recognize the needs of mothers, for example by providing crèche facilities or maternity protection, and few women will find themselves in this relatively comfortable position. And the fact that lone mothers are likely to be concentrated in low-paid employment is reflected in the 136,000 such mothers who in April 1992 received family credit benefit as a supplement to their earnings (NCOPF 1993). When the factors of limited work opportunities, low wages and poor childcare facilities are combined it is all too easy to see how lone mothers are frequently disadvantaged by their maternal obligations. Eekelaar and Maclean, in a pre-Child Support Act study, found that the effects of divorce on lone mothers would be felt in respect of income, with a general movement into poverty by those with dependent children (1986: 67–73). While the study refers to the period before the Child Support Act's implementation, the structural factors considered by the research remain unimproved to any great extent. As more recent research has shown, there may be a number of factors that affect the lone mother's decision to work outside the home. For some, the practical day-to-day care of their children will be more important than financial provision through employment in the public sphere. Edwards and Duncan suggest that the solutions put forward to tackle lone mothers' low participation in the labour market in Britain are based upon a 'simple stimulus–response model of social action'. This involves the model of a 'rational economic man', who calculates their welfare based on cost–benefit calculations. Social policy makers assume that if stimuli such as benefit levels, tax allowances and childcare provision for lone mothers are appropriately amended lone mothers will take up paid work (Edwards and Duncan 1996: 115). However, as the authors demonstrate, lone mothers' decisions are influenced by particular 'gendered moral rationalities', which are contextually specific and different from those based on the individual economic rationale model (*ibid.*: 115–16). Their decision making will be affected by norms shared by others in their social network and by other members of their social group and will not necessarily fit the model of economic rationality (*ibid.*: 120). Recent Labour government commitments to providing aid for childcare through the working families tax credit scheme may not provide the necessary incentive for lone mothers to re-enter the labour force.[11] Moreover, as I will explore later, lone mothers will find themselves caught in a network of conflicting messages about the practical support of their children.

The Conservative government responsible for introducing the new system of child support may have derived satisfaction from its success in striking a balance between old and new families. However, the practical effect in a vast number of these cases was to bring both sets of families to or below the poverty level, with the mother of the former family standing to gain nothing financially. At the same time, her former partner and his new family were likely to be made worse off as a result of agency intervention. The newly formed families were subjected to greater financial pressure, which sometimes placed the second family under a great deal of stress. There was a perceived fear of new families being forced onto state benefits if the financial strain was to lead to their disintegration.

The Conservative government initially chose to ignore a recommendation made by the Social Security Committee to incorporate some provision beyond a safety net for step-families on the basis that step-parents assumed an important function in reducing the number of lone parent families (Social Security Committee 1994: para. 81). The Conservative government later reconsidered its position on step-families in the White Paper *Improving Child Support*, where it announced that from April 1995 the Child Support Agency would allow reasonable housing costs in full for new partners and their children (HMSO 1995: para. 3.10). This

---

11. The childcare tax credit is intended to meet 70 per cent of eligible childcare costs up to a maximum of £100 per week for one child and £150 per week for two or more children. The scheme came into effect in October 1999.

change benefited the step-family and resulted in a lower award for the first family. More significantly, the new measure signalled a marked retreat from the policy that biological children take priority over step-children, and to some extent it re-established the importance of the concept of the child of the family. The new measure can be regarded as a means of recognizing and rewarding the man who has taken on the responsibility of a step-family. In other words, the father who can be constructed as fulfilling the dual role of financially supporting his own biological children and his step-children will receive government approval for his twofold responsibility. He is a good father in law twice over. The present Labour government also recognizes this, through recognizing the cost of step-children and by its intention to reduce overall his child support obligation to the children of his first family (see further, Mostyn 1999: 98). The Labour government's most recent proposals for reform clearly attempt to address the concerns of families with step-children. The White Paper announced that any maintenance for step-children coming into the reconstituted family will be ignored in the calculation of the non-residential father's percentage rate for maintenance for the first family (HMSO 1999: 3 of 8). Clearly, Labour social policy may well come to advantage second families when the biological parents of children in second families provide well for their children, but at a cost to children of first families with no new additional wage earner. While it can be argued that the Labour government is responding to failures of the original legislation, it has also deviated from the principle of parity between first and subsequent families.

It has become apparent that there are very real dangers implicit in talking 'principles', and by this I mean prioritizing the principle as the focal point for the debate on lone mothers' poverty over and above the diversity of the experiences of women as the subjects of poverty. This is not to say that talk about principles should be abandoned but rather that, in debating the subject of lone mothers' poverty, academics, practitioners and legislators should consider the direct implications of these principles for those who experience poverty. This can only be achieved by examining the principle in the context of how it is embodied in the Act, how it operates in practice, and by considering the practical ramifications for those to whom it applies.

And when the principle is examined in relation to the position of the parent with care, it becomes obvious that it operates, in practice, to benefit only two main groups. The first group constitutes those lone mothers who are in receipt of state benefits and whose ex-partners earned substantial enough sums of money to raise their incomes well above the state benefit rate. The second group that the principle may benefit is women who are employed in the labour market and do not have to rely on the state benefit system. Any maintenance paid to them will supplement their earnings. Only in cases where the non-residential parent is in a very high income bracket does the lone parent benefit in any substantial way. It was speculated at the time of implementation that less than one in ten lone parents would benefit financially from the new legislation (Walker 1993: 92). Of the half a million cases dealt with by the agency from April to September 1993, there were only 20,000 non-benefit cases in which the carer kept the whole sum. What becomes apparent when the principle is examined in its practical context is that it is ineffective in ameliorating the lives of those who constitute the poorest and most vulnerable in our society.

It is my opinion that the danger in talking only of 'principles' in debates on lone mothers' poverty is that the mass of contradictions in the power relations, interests and experiences of women's lives with regard to poverty are allowed to be forgotten, ignored or trivialized. For debates on poverty to be politically relevant to women, they should strive to recognize the importance of experience in constituting the meaning of women's practical realities. It remains far too early to assess the likely impact of the Labour government's proposals for the child support legislation. However, the government does seem to have taken more notice of the protestations of middle-class men required to pay increased sums of maintenance rather than of the problems encountered by lone mothers in securing and receiving regular maintenance. Feminist researchers should seek at all costs not to undermine or perhaps worsen, even evacuate, women's subjective experiences, because they provide a useful source for understanding how power relations are structured in society. Moreover, they provide women, whether they wear the badge of feminism or not, with the impetus and desire for social change.

I have noted how through talking and prioritizing principles there is a very real danger of evacuating the subject, for principles cannot take into account the diversity of women's experiences of class, race, ethnicity, religion and sexual affiliation. I have noted the value of interviewing as a means of incorporating experience into the research project. But the interview as a technique has been problematized, for only through problematization can research be improved through striving to ensure that the lessons that have been learned through practical activities are heeded. This section serves as a reminder to others engaged in work about or with women that women in all diversity are the subjects we should be concerned with in debates on the subject of poverty. Lest we forget.

chapter 2

Dissident mothers

Sure Start is taking an entirely new approach, which
recognises that *the family* forms the very foundation and
building block for children's future success in both social
life and in educational achievement.

(Blunkett 1999: 1 of 8, my italics)

David Blunkett, Education and Employment Secretary, announces a
new stage of what the Labour government terms a 'programme of investment in children and the family' (1999: 1 of 8). 'The family' has long been
an area upon which there has been cross-party concern. The current government continues to identify 'the family' as the potential source and site
of the solution to society's troubles. However, exactly what constitutes
'the family' is often not explicitly stated but rather assumed. While 'the
family' is perceived as foundational to children and society's success, an
articulation of the constitution of family often only comes into play when
a particular family form deviates from the assumed model. While our
experiences of family life are multifarious, including lone parent families, lesbian and homosexual families, heterosexual families, and extended
families, 'the family' as traditionally constructed with two heterosexual parents (preferably married) and children is the form referred to in the above
statement. As Finch has argued, the traditional nuclear family is the dominant family in terms of what counts as 'real' family. She states: 'in terms
of beliefs, values and images the dominance of this family form has by
no means been undermined. If anything its dominance is growing, as politicians of various persuasions talk about "strengthening family life" ' (Finch
1996: 15). 'The family' that politicians are concerned with strengthening

is one very specific model against which other forms are measured and adjudicated. Lord Irvine, the Labour government's Lord Chancellor, stated the commitment to marriage thus: 'This Government believes that marriage is the best way for two adults to share their lives and raise their children. We do have a duty to support marriage' (Lord Irvine 1999).

Clearly, the Labour government is concerned with protecting and promoting marriage as the institution most suited to accommodating the needs of children. Thus, the government does not shy away from the prescriptive approach to families that so predominated during the early 1990s from the Conservative government. The articulation about what constitutes the ideal family form is brought about by socio-political concerns about the perceived disintegration of 'the family'. In the legal arena, policy behind the law regulating aspects of family life and the legislation itself occasionally specifically refers to particular types of family grouping. As Diduck has noted regarding the Child Support Act 1991, policy behind the Act 'speaks most directly to lone-parent families, and the words "lone-parent" are necessary to set these families apart from unmodified ones, on which the Act does not purport to concentrate' (Diduck 1995: 527–8). Groupings other than the traditional nuclear family are thus rendered different and moreover defective. Political rhetoric that states a preference for this kind of family also ensures that this differentiation projects a form of deviancy upon those families failing to conform to the ideal. The construction of the traditional family as the paradigmatic form serves to marginalize those groupings that may well regard themselves as family. Women seeking to parent alone are viewed with suspicion and indeed some fear as they are also often blamed in part for the disintegration of 'the family'.

During the whole of the 1990s, there was much fervent social and legal debate over what came to be perceived as women's increasing willingness to have and raise children alone. Among right-wing politicians in particular, there was an extremely vilificatory attitude towards women who elected to parent single-handedly (or with another woman) and towards men who were concomitantly regarded as absconding from their paternal duties. Many of these debates emanated from a political concern about the lone parents' reliance on social security benefits and how the then Conservative government could reduce public expenditure. Others stemmed from concerns brought about by advances in reproductive technologies, which created the potential for a new kind of 'fatherless' family. While both lone mothers and non-residential fathers were constructed in a negative manner in these debates, the lone mother headed household became the embodiment of the contemporary 'social problem' of child support, which involved financial, social and emotional components. This chapter is concerned with the correlative implications of the concept of father 'absence' for the mother who either elects to parent with another woman or who chooses or is forced to parent alone. It is clear that lesbian mothers may not be lone mothers in the sense that they are raising children single-handedly. However, I argue that lesbian mothers who obtain unlicensed donor inseminations are treated for child support purposes as if their lesbian partner did not exist. I therefore unearth the ways in which social, political and legal debates about motherhood and child support have evolved to include the dominant idea that mothers must ensure as far as possible that a child has a *father* to participate in her/his life. This is shown in the second section, where I discuss the construction of the never-married mother.

This chapter is therefore concerned with unearthing the various ways in which mothers who are perceived as wilfully keeping the father from the child are constructed and responded to within social, political and legal discourse. To some extent, my separation of the categories of lone mothers is an arbitrary one, as clearly there may be overlaps between the classifications. In doing so, I repeat a pattern established by others interested in the subject of lone motherhood. The classification of lone mothers is frequently made by activists and other commentators who seek to campaign for or are concerned to portray lone mothers in a more sympathetic light than many of those participating in the less than favourable mainstream debates: for example, the National Council for One Parent Families (hereafter NCOPF), which in its annual report 1994–5 states that in 1993 60 per cent of lone mothers were divorced, separated or widowed. Additionally, while 40 per cent of lone mothers were classed as single (i.e. never-married) most births outside marriage (55 per cent) were registered by both parents living at the same address. This suggests a large proportion of never-married lone mothers did not choose to have a child alone but, rather, made the decision as a partner in a cohabiting couple that later broke up. Additionally, the NCOPF noted that the number of births to unmarried teenagers has declined since 1990. *The Independent* newspaper (6 July 1993) broke down single parents into several distinct groups, noting that 70 per cent of lone parents were 'mature' men and women who had been married and become lone parents through death, separation or divorce. The remaining 30 per cent, the paper claimed, comprised young lone mothers, but 'contrary to popular view, the fastest-growing group of single parents is not teenagers but those between 20 and 24'. The paper also cited the statistic that 65 per cent of lone mothers were once married to the fathers of their children. The paper also cites the statistic that of the 845,000 lone parents claiming income support, only 45,000 are 16- to 19-year-olds. Marina

Warner cites the statistic that 65 per cent of lone mothers were once married to the fathers of their children (1994: 12).

Lone mothers are classified in several ways, often depending on the means by which they eventually come to parent alone. Some women will choose to parent alone or to co-parent with a same-sex partner. Others will become lone mothers as a result of widowhood or divorce, while some will become mothers while in a cohabiting situation. The second two examples may have attained the status of lone motherhood through the breakdown of a long-term relationship. The potential for overlap of the categories is clear. For example, women who separate from or divorce their partners can be both lesbian and determined to end the heterosexual relationship. Notwithstanding that it is not until the woman's sexuality becomes visible to others, who may construct her sexuality as problematic, the mother in question will come to be seen as wilfully abandoning heterosexuality and therefore dangerous. The distinction remains conceptually useful for the analysis of the automatic assumptions that are frequently made about never-married and lesbian mothers wilfully renouncing the heterosexual. There is a tendency in debates on lone motherhood for the heterosexual separated, divorced and especially widowed mothers to be portrayed in a more sympathetic light, particularly if the mother can be represented as coming to lone motherhood through no fault of her own.

Statistics are useful in revealing the demographics of lone motherhood. Also, they provide a political tool for those seeking to defend the rights of lone mothers to adequate financial and social support. Campaigners use the statistics to correct the much-vaunted illusion that the rising numbers of lone mothers are mainly 'feckless' teenagers who get pregnant deliberately in order to secure public housing. For example, *The Guardian* stated in 1995 how David Shaw, then vice-chairman of the backbench Finance Committee, had suggested that no benefit be paid to 'any young mother who could not produce a marriage certificate'. He was quoted as saying: 'Why are children born where a proper, stable relationship hasn't been established?' (14 August 1995). In the same article, John Redwood was reported as saying that in cases where the father of a child could not be traced, the next option would be to look to the extended family for support. He stated: 'if no one in the family can help, maybe the girl should consider letting a couple adopt her child to provide the home her baby needs'. Sue Slipman, the former director of NCOPF, stated in *The Independent* that 'public opinion tends to lump these single parents together, seeing them as a mass of young – probably teenage – mothers who have become pregnant through carelessness and chosen fecklessly to have their child "on the state"' (*The Independent*, 6 July 1993).

   This chapter is concerned with contemporary social and legal representations of the lesbian mother, the never-married heterosexual mother
and the teenage mother. The first group of mothers to be considered is
composed of women who can be constructed as wilfully rejecting heterosexuality – lesbians. When women are constructed as rejecting heterosexuality *per se*, the law responds in a manner that seeks to restrict women's
ability to make the decision to parent without a man. In the attempt to
contain women's determination to parent with another woman, the law
is also constructing lesbian mothers as contravening one of society's
most valorized conventions – 'the family'. The law firmly places lesbian
mothers on the margins of society as they are constructed as not 'proper'
family. Section 28 of the Local Government Act 1988 renders lesbian and
homosexual families as 'pretend' families and therefore not proper family. They are not 'proper' families in two senses: first, lesbian and homosexual families are not proper in the sense that they are constructed by
discourse as in some sense an incorrect or irregular family form; second,
and relatedly, they are represented as not proper in a moral sense. Lesbian
and homosexual families are rendered deviant, indecent, improper and
incapable of performing to the same level as the traditional heterosexual
family. Specific aspects of the law governing access to reproductive technologies restrict access to artificial insemination. The standard by which
women are adjudged 'fit' for treatment is either their ability to provide a
father for the child or the financial means to support a child throughout
her life. While the measures used are restrictive, they do not necessarily
preclude the possibility of single or lesbian women gaining access to treatment. But, as will be demonstrated, it is likely that treatment will be effectively limited to middle-class women as they are likelier to fulfil the criteria
of demonstrating their ability to support a child financially in the absence
of a male breadwinner. Working-class and unemployed women are therefore marginalized because of the unlikelihood of their being able to
demonstrate their capacity to provide financially.

The case of the lesbian mother

No need for a man about the house.

(*The Guardian*, 2 July 1994)

   The headline above refers to an unreported High Court decision to
grant a lesbian couple a joint residence order of their 22-month-old son
under the Children Act 1989. The judge presiding over the case granted

the residence order on the grounds that the child's welfare was his 'first and paramount consideration, and that the evidence pointed over-whelmingly to the making of the order' (*The Pink Paper*, July 1994). The order has the effect of granting joint parental responsibility to both the parents, and in the event of death or the breakdown of the relationship both women will retain parental responsibility for the child as per the Children Act 1989, section 12(2). Given the law's history of antipathy towards homosexual and lesbian parents, the case can be construed as an instance of a more sympathetic approach towards lesbian parenting. However, the decision should be viewed with cautious optimism. One good decision does not represent evidence of a more general trend towards an enlightened approach to lesbian and gay parenting. Much of the research conducted upon judicial attitudes towards gay and lesbian parents where custody is at issue focuses upon the competing claims of lesbian mothers and heterosexual fathers.[1] It is worth noting that in this case there is no competing claim by a heterosexual father who can offer the law's preferred alternative of a traditional nuclear family form.

It would appear at first sight then that the case has little if anything to do with fathers at all. Here is a case concerning two caring female parents who want to ensure continuity of parental responsibility throughout their child's life. The biological father, a friend who had donated his sperm in an informal arrangement between the couple and himself, had signed papers stating that he wanted no responsibility for raising the child (*The Pink Paper*, July 1994). It is clear therefore that the lesbian couple and the biological father were keen to write his contribution out of the family's life. Notwithstanding the family's fierce determination to keep the male actor out of the picture, the government determines to bring the biological father's contribution back onto the legal, social and political agendas. This insistence on enforcing the biological relationship between child and sperm donor conflicts with the position in relation to licensed treatment. Under the Human Fertilisation and Embryology Act 1990 (hereafter HFEA), any donor who willingly gives his sperm in an agreement not sanctioned by the National Health Service or a licensed infertility clinic will be regarded as the father of the child and as such will be liable for financial maintenance. If the treatment is licensed and the partner who has no genetic link to the child consents to the administration of the donor

---

1.   See, for example, the work of S. Boyd, which demonstrates the judicial preference for heterosexual, two-parent families in contested custody cases involving lesbian mothers (1992); Beresford 1994; Arnup 1989.

insemination then he will be treated as the parent of the child for child support purposes (HFEA 1990: sections 28(3) and 29(1)). In summary, the sperm donor who operates within the legally defined framework will not be regarded as a parent, while the donor who operates outside the guidelines runs the risk of being pursued by the Child Support Agency for financial maintenance.

The law's apparent schizophrenia on the importance of the biological relation stems from a concern to ensure that the rules on reproductive technologies replicate as far as possible the traditional nuclear family. Fatherhood attained by consent rather than biology stands in contrast to the law's emphasis upon the biological link in informal arrangements. Alistair Burt (then a junior social security minister) made a House of Commons statement about the court's decision, stating: 'There can be no private arrangements which leave the taxpayers picking up the bill . . . It is right to pursue the biological father, and the CSA will do so' (*The Pink Paper*, July 1994). The use of the word 'taxpayer' serves to emphasize that where a 'private' arrangement has been made between the mother and the sperm donor there is a wider public interest in ensuring that the donor is held responsible for the child's upkeep rather than the state. The Child Support Agency is called upon to guarantee that financial responsibility for the child remains within the realm of the private arrangement. The reference to 'private arrangements' refers to the manner in which the donor insemination came about by informal means – i.e. outside the legally regulated system under the National Health Service or through a licensed private infertility clinic. Under limited circumstances, the law will recognize the value of attributing fatherhood status to the man who consents to artificial insemination. In cases where there is no man willing to stand as the father of the child, the law will seek to enforce the relation because of the perceived threat to the traditional social order whereby men are held responsible for children's upkeep. In the case referred to above, the law refuses to see the relationship between the two mothers as capable of replacing the 'natural' paternal relation. Smart describes the law's position thus:

> The law appears to be moving in two conflicting directions at the same time. In the case of divorce and [single motherhood], there is a growing emphasis on the importance of biological fatherhood and paternity. In the case of AID, however, the opposite is occurring and the legal concept of the 'child of the family' seems to ignore the importance of legal paternity altogether.   (1987: 114)

There is some truth in what Smart says when it is related to the legal approach to licensed treatment. However, the situation regarding unlicensed insemination is more complicated than Smart's either/or approach suggests. When treatment is unlicensed, the law insists on forging at least some connection between the biological father and the child. In this case, the law is concerned with ensuring financial responsibility for the child, but if the law insisted on imposing legal liability for maintenance upon the biological progenitor a concomitant would be enhancing the possibility of the assertion of paternal rights over the child. The implication is that the legal regulation of reproductive technologies tends to favour a particular family structure, namely the stable heterosexual relationship. Where women are determined to become mothers alone or with other women, the law is stringent in allowing access to and sanctioning treatments.

The framework provided by the HFEA serves to restrict the practice of informal private arrangements. Lesbians who use informal methods may suffer the disadvantages of a future challenge by the biological father for parental responsibility and/or harassment by the Child Support Agency to name the sperm donor. Notwithstanding, lesbians may well feel that informal arrangements are the best possible option available to them, as the HFEA posits another restriction upon the access to licensed treatment. Section 13(5) of the Act states:

> A woman shall not be provided with treatment services unless account has been taken of the welfare of any child who may be born as a result of the treatment (including the need of that child for a father), and of any other child who may be affected by the birth.

In addition to the above statutory provision, the Human Fertilisation and Embryology Authority, which is the statutory licensing body established by the HFEA, outlines guidelines in its code of practice for consultation relating to artificial insemination. Section 3.16(b) states:

> Centres are required to have regard to the child's need for a father and should pay particular attention to the prospective mother's ability to meet the child's needs throughout his or her childhood and where appropriate, whether there is anyone else within the prospective mother's family and social circle who is willing and able to share the responsibility for meeting those needs and for bringing up, maintaining and caring for the child.

It is possible to argue that the authority's code of practice guidelines leave interpretative space for some lesbians to request treatment on the basis that they have a stable relationship and that their partner can contribute to the responsibility for the raising of the child. However, poorer women unable to secure treatment on the National Health Service and/or who are unable to demonstrate that their partner can contribute to the child's upbringing may be discriminated against, at least on the grounds that they cannot afford to raise the child.

As Cooper and Herman note, 'the white, middle class, "coupled" lesbian, with a well-paid, secure job and a spacious home, may well be more likely to receive "treatment services" than the ex-prostitute refused them in one recent case' (1991: 78). However, section 16(b) of the code of practice still gives priority to the relationship between a heterosexual man and woman, despite the opening out of the possibility of establishing a case for treatment on the basis of support other than paternal support. There is no acknowledgement of any alternative family form other than a reference to the mother's own family having the potential to offer support. As such, the law denies the potential existence of alternative family forms. In short, if a prospective mother presents herself without a father for her child then she should be treated with caution. A fatherless family is no fit family. This view is evident in the Warnock Report, which preceded the HFEA. In it, Mary Warnock states:

> We believe that as a general rule it is better for children to be born
> into a two-parent family, with both a father and a mother, although
> we recognize that it is impossible to predict with any certainty how
> lasting such a relationship will be.   (1985: 11–12)

The conjunction of father and mother in Mary Warnock's statement serves to affirm the nuclear family. Conservative MPs reiterated the ferocity with which Warnock supports the traditional family form in the aftermath of the decision relating to the ascription of the joint residence order to the lesbian couple mentioned above. Emma Nicholson, then Conservative MP for West Devon and Torridge, said:

> I'm immensely unhappy when adult sexual behaviour inflicts a
> distorted lifestyle on children. Every child is born of a mother and
> a father and I strenuously believe that every child deserves a mother
> and a father.   (cited in *The Independent*, 30 June 1994)

Not only does Nicholson affirm the nuclear family but she also reduces the women's relationship to a purely sexual one and ignores the capacity for two women to rear a child as a family unit. It is clear from much of the rhetoric about artificial insemination by donor (AID) that lesbian relationships are widely regarded as being generally undesirable and incapable of replacing the heterosexual nuclear family. In this way, the regulation of AID procedures can be seen as creating a hierarchy of sexual relationships, with the heterosexual relationship clearly being assigned the dominant position. Furthermore, by creating a hierarchy of families based upon sexual orientation, the family is reduced to a means of containing sexual behaviour. Lesbians are barred from marriage and therefore remain outside the state-legitimated family form. And so, the refusal to sanction lesbian and homosexual relationships through marriage stands as a reminder that their sexual behaviour remains outside the realms of 'normal' sexual and family life. Because of the 'abnormality' of their sexual lives, lesbians can never meet the ideal of the traditional nuclear family.

For child support purposes, when the donor insemination of a lesbian mother has been procured by informal, unlicensed means, the biological father of the child may be held legally accountable for the financial upkeep of the child. In these cases, the lesbian relationship is rendered to all intents and purposes null and void. Even in cases where treatment is obtained through a licensed clinic, lesbians may feel forced to conceal their sexuality in order to procure treatment, as will be revealed in the next section. The government justifies its stance on unlicensed treatment through the notion that there is a public interest in making the biological father pay. The 'taxpayer' is once again called upon in order to emphasize that there is a public interest in making the father pay. Lesbian families are constructed as being outside the remit of the public interest. Poorer lesbian families are particularly marginalized by policy on insemination and by discourses on child support. Lesbians are still denied access to the state-legitimated relationship of marriage, and they remain for many purposes on the margins of society.

No sex for the single mother

In Emma Nicholson's tirade against the lesbian family, she also stresses the biological necessity for both a mother and a father and thus emphasizes that as far as biology is concerned there can be no such thing as a fatherless child. This view is also apparent in the House of Lords debate on the Child Support Bill. Lord Stoddart, voicing his concerns over the administration of AID to single women, tabled an amendment to 'equalise the position and to ensure that the taxpayer is in the same position whether a child is conceived naturally or through AID' (*Hansard* 1990–91: cols 386–8). He is referring to the possibility of single women obtaining AID treatment in licensed clinics, which guarantees anonymity for the sperm donor, thus (for child support purposes) exempting him from being pursued for maintenance for his biological child. He states:

Since the publication of the Bill, it has come to light that certain clinics are administering AID to single women who have no male partner and *intend* not to have one. As a result, there will be only one parent with financial responsibility. However, there is a father involved – the donor of the sperm – but because he wishes merely to perpetuate his genes, without any human relationship with the mother of his child and without any responsibility for the child's upbringing, he is to escape all financial responsibility for the child's nurture and care . . . A father is a father irrespective of the method used to fertilise a woman's ovum, and there is no case for different treatment.   (*Hansard* 1990–91: cols 389–90)

Lord Stoddart, in tabling his amendment, is clearly fearful of an upsurge in single women seeking AID treatment with the intention of never having a man in their lives. Later in his speech, it becomes clear that his prime concern is the possibility that at some point in her lifetime a single woman may be unable to support her child financially. In choosing to parent alone, she fails to provide the child, the government and the taxpayer with any financial back-up should circumstances lead to her inability to support the child. Stoddart's concern lies not only with the idea that women may become free to parent without a man. He also stresses the desire to have a father held financially responsible for any resulting child's upkeep.

According to Stoddart's formulation, a sperm donor should assume all the responsibilities of a father as traditionally construed. He shows disapprobation for the biological father, who, he alleges, seeks to perpetuate his genes without assuming any of the ongoing responsibilities normally associated with fatherhood. In other words, Lord Stoddart constructs the biological father who donates sperm as feckless, irresponsible and selfish. He is also concerned that the advances in reproductive technologies give rise to the possibility of men perpetuating their genes without having to assume the traditional responsibilities associated therewith. In his scenario, the woman who elects to parent alone is constructed as wilful and therefore a threat to the social order. In contrast, the sperm donor is constituted as spineless and as shirking moral responsibility.

Stoddart is determined to establish that biology equates with fatherhood, but this idea is foolish given that the law has long accepted the concept of the social father and the concept of the 'child of the family', particularly in relation to licensed AID. After debate, Stoddart's amendment was withdrawn, it being stated that the statutory framework provided by the HFEA and the guidelines of the code of practice are adequate to regulate access to treatment. It was argued by the then Lord Chancellor that the number of cases of single women gaining access to treatment would be few, as the child's need for a father was to be considered before giving treatment. Additionally, the Lord Chancellor reiterated that when women make informal arrangements they may be forced to furnish the Child Support Agency with the requisite information to trace the biological father (*Hansard* 1990–91: cols 389–90). The Lord Chancellor expected the guidelines to be interpreted strictly, with single women being discriminated against on the grounds that they may fail to provide their child with a father. In other words, a woman who is unable to demonstrate a willingness to incorporate a father into the child's life may face considerable difficulty in securing licensed treatment. It is suggested that a sufficient block to women obtaining licensed treatment is their perceived wilfulness in seeking to parent without a man.

Nineteenth-century legislation sought to regulate women's perceived unruly sexual behaviour (Smart 1992: 7–32). In contrast, the HFEA 1990 and its associated code of practice is concerned more particularly with the regulation of women's *biological* capacity to have children without sexual relations with men. In other words, the emphasis of the legislation is upon the perceived need to manage women's biological ability to procreate without a legal father. There is evidence of a strong concern about how the development of new reproductive technology has the capacity to separate biological reproduction from heterosexuality and its concomitant norms and traditions. The innovative technology of artificial insemination, which is capable of reducing parenthood to a biological function, is perceived as a threat to the existing social order, which places the highest value on the heterosexual act and the paternal relation. The legislation is concerned with containing women's constructed unruly biological capacity. That is not to say, however, that the legislation is not at all concerned with the control of women's sexuality. But, rather than being concerned with the *containment* of inappropriate sexual behaviour, the legislation seeks to *promote* women's procreative behaviour through the more 'natural' route of heterosexual intercourse, thus promoting the heterosexual model of human relationships at the same time as marginalizing the lesbian relationship.

The extent to which lesbians would openly present their sexual orientation when seeking AID treatment is open to question. In an article that draws upon her own personal experiences of attempting to obtain AID treatment in Canada, Katherine Arnup recounts that originally she had no intention of revealing her sexual orientation as a lesbian when seeking insemination from a registered clinic. Arnup felt that she would receive resistance to her request if it were known that she was either a single woman or a lesbian. She believed that there would be less opposition if she presented herself as a heterosexual single woman, and this is the option she originally chose. However, she disclosed herself as a lesbian in the preliminary interview as the result of an attack of nerves. Her request for treatment was refused. The doctor concerned claimed that her 'homosexuality had nothing whatsoever to do with the decision . . . It is the policy of this clinic not to inseminate single people, regardless of their sex . . . or their sexual . . . bias' (Arnup 1994: 99).

Anxious to deny that Arnup's lesbianism had influenced the refusal, the doctor makes the claim that clinic policy is not to inseminate single people 'regardless of their sex or sexual bias'. Despite the employment of the generic 'people' the doctor is necessarily only talking about women, as it is women and not men who are inseminated. Failure to use 'women' and 'lesbians' paradoxically highlights (because of the absurdity of the statement) that the case involves women and not men. In relation to the practice of insemination by donor, the person seeking treatment will inevitably be a woman.

In England in the early 1990s, the press reported instances of single women seeking assisted reproduction at licensed clinics as 'virgin' births. The press constructed the incidents as to do with women renouncing sexual intercourse with men. And the condition of virginity is loaded with meaning through a normative heterosexual narrative of penile penetration. It was unclear at the outset of the 'virgin birth' controversy as to whether the 'virgins' in question were heterosexual or lesbian (Cooper and Herman 1991). But it is noted by Cooper and Herman that at least one of the single women requesting treatment presented herself as heterosexual. According to the above authors, the psychotherapist involved in one of the cases discussed in a feature in *The Guardian* stated that a woman putting herself forward for insemination had no history of sexual activity and had no intention of becoming involved in a sexual relationship. The psychotherapist was cited as saying:

> The patient saw nothing unusual in her request. She believed that medical technology would provide the answer to all her dreams, and she pictured her future life with a perfect child. She believed she would be a good parent and this would be jeopardised if she married the wrong man . . . Are such women genuinely reluctant to enter into a sexual relationship, yet want a child? In some cases I doubt whether having a child is the primary motivation.
>
> (*The Guardian*, 12 March 1991)

The passage indicates that the psychotherapist finds it difficult to come to terms with the fact that a woman could possibly want a child but not a sexual relationship. I suggest that the psychotherapist's difficulty in coming to terms with the fact that a woman might not want sex is a consequence of the centrality of penetration to the economy of heterosexuality.[2] The idea is so ingrained that it is difficult to imagine life without penile penetration.

Moreover, the psychotherapist seems to suggest that the woman in question is deluding herself with regard to her ability to raise a child without the help of a man. He doubts the woman's primary motivation for having the treatment, thus questioning her mental capacity and the grounds for her making the decision to seek treatment. The author's allusion to the woman's delusion is consistent with contemporary observations of psychiatric practices, which construct and emphasize women's mind/body instability.[3] The woman seeking treatment is cited as saying that her parenting ability would be jeopardized if she were to choose to marry the 'wrong man'. For the purposes of child support and the concept of ongoing parental responsibility, it matters little that she associates herself with the 'wrong man', for any man will do as long as a biological and/or a legally binding association can be established.

Clinics adopting the policy that artificial insemination should not as a general rule be freely available to the single woman are unlikely to be sympathetic to women who renounce men through their lesbianism or reject men on the basis that they would prefer to parent alone. Such stringent policies on the administration of artificial insemination serve both an ideological and a practical function. Ideologically, the policy perpetuates the notion that a child should have and needs a father and a mother. For practical purposes, the policy limits the number of single and lesbian women who are able to gain access to treatment from licensed clinics and so gain exemption from divulging information about the child's biological father for child support purposes.

Despite the social and legal limitations placed upon lesbians and single women, it is clear that artificial insemination by donor does have the capacity to create a new category of 'fatherless' children. The potential

---

2. See further Collier (1992), who argues that there are five assumptions around sexual intercourse in law: sex is natural; what is natural is heterosexual; genital sex is primary and determining; 'true' sexual intercourse is phallocentric; and sex is something that takes place in marriage.

3. For a study of psychiatric evidence offered about women in criminal law trials, see Allen 1987.

to dispense with fathers is clearly a matter of concern for many commentators. In 1981, a British report, *The Artificial Family*, noted that 'AID could become a means of dispensing with marriage and the inconvenience of a husband and, of course, with a father too' (Snowden and Mitchell 1981: 119). For example, in cases such as the above where a woman without a male partner is successful in obtaining licensed treatment, the child is to all intents and purposes without a father. The perceived exclusion from families of men as fathers and all that is associated with the beneficial aspects of the father/child relationship is a point to which I return and develop in Chapter 4. Reproductive technologies permit the fracturing of the significant family tie of sexual affiliation, which is given primacy and privileged through the legal institution of marriage. Underpinning the privileged status of the heterosexual family is the idea of the naturalness of the form.

The dominance of this family form serves to render the 'unnatural' family – the homosexual, lesbian relationship or single woman – as being incapable of providing the 'right' kind of support and role model for children. If the heterosexual family is defined as 'natural', then anything seen as different is automatically rendered as 'Other' or unnatural to it. If marriage is seen as the most appropriate institution in which to raise children, and lesbians and homosexual fathers are denied access to the institution, there is an underlying presumption in the ban that lesbians and gay men will be unable to meet children's needs and societal expectations. As Fineman so eloquently writes of the US context:

> children's problems are deemed to be created by the fact that they are 'trapped' in a 'deviant' family situation, 'prisoners' or 'victims' of a family that is often 'broken' through divorce or 'pathological' in that it was never sanctified by marriage . . . The sexually affiliated family is the imposed ideal and, as such, it escapes sustained, serious consideration and criticism.   (1995: 147)

When Fineman speaks of the 'sexually affiliated family', she is talking about a specific affiliation between heterosexual men and women. Lesbians and single women who seek to or are constructed as renouncing the heterosexual affiliation model and the possibility of a paternal contribution to their child's upbringing are conceived of as outside 'real' family life. Despite the court's recent decision to award a joint residence order to a lesbian couple noted in the previous section, statutory guidelines are such as to discourage single heterosexual and lesbian women from seeking licensed treatment for artificial insemination in the first place. As a result, many women will elect to travel the route of informal arrangements in order to have children.

Arnup's article (1994) is instructive on the way that US courts have striven to enforce the link between the donor of the semen and the child conceived by informal artificial insemination when the biological father has sought to establish his paternity rights over the objections of the mother. In five out of the six cases examined by Arnup, the courts affirmed the paternal rights and obligations of the sperm donor. The implications for women who seek to expand upon their reproductive powers and assume alternative family forms by informal means are obvious.

If English law follows the example of the USA, lesbians and hetero-sexual single women who use informal methods of conception run the risk of having their family lives upset by laws determined to guarantee male responsibility for children even when women, for whatever reason, forsake it. Alistair Burt made it clear under the Conservative government that the Child Support Agency would pursue the biological father for maintenance when informal arrangements have been made. The former government's message was made clearly; and the present government's approach to informal treatment remains the same at present. Women using informal means are not allowed to raise children without the minimum of support from the male progenitors of their children if the treatment has not been sanctioned by a state-legitimated organ such as a licensed fertility clinic. There is no sign as yet of any change of government policy in this area. While formal treatment is not exclusively denied to single women and lesbians, whether coupled or not, once again it will be only those women who can demonstrate a relatively stable financial back-ground who are likely to gain access to treatment in licensed clinics.

Women's wilfulness to parent alone or with a same-sex partner is not sufficient to secure their autonomy either within the realm of the reproductive or within the law on child support. There is a strong link between financial independence and the reproductive autonomy of women. If women can successfully establish their financial independence, they might then be allowed the freedom to procreate and raise children without a readily discernible father to hold financially responsible for the child. As such, women's freedom to have children without a legally identifiable father is hindered by preventing their access to state-legitimated treatment or by attempting to hold the sperm donor financially respons-ible under the Child Support Act once a child is conceived as a result of informal arrangements.

When lesbian mothers elect to adopt informal insemination arrange-ments, they place themselves in danger of being harassed by the Child Support Agency for the details of their child's biological father. In the main, however, lesbian mothers have escaped widespread vilification in many of the general debates about the particular issue of child support.[4] The same cannot be said for young mothers, who are constructed as being all too willing to embrace heterosexual relations without the confines of a marriage relationship. In the ensuing section, I will examine how the press has reported stories involving young unmarried mothers. It will be argued that young lone mothers are constituted as a destructive force in relation to their reproductive capacity. The representation of lone mothers as destructive stands in stark contrast to the more traditional association of a mother's *productivity* with regard to her procreative and mothering capacities. Young mothers are constructed as deviants who elect to form unnatural alliances with the state rather than with the fathers of their children. They are also constructed as being incapable of raising children successfully and as responsible for the destruction of the fabric of society.

The case of the teenage mother

Statistics show that 'teenage' lone mothers constitute only a very small proportion of all lone mothers in receipt of state benefits. Nevertheless, it would appear from many of the statements generated by right-wing politicians during the latter part of the 1990s that this small group of women constitutes the biggest threat to society. For example, in the summer of 1995 John Redwood, then Secretary of State for Wales, renewed an attack on lone mothers that he had started two years earlier when visiting a Welsh housing estate. His vitriolic assault on lone mothers had not at all changed over the two-year period. Redwood was critical of the support given to lone mothers, and he was quoted as saying in *The Guardian*: 'The assumption is that the illegitimate child is the passport to a council flat and a benefit income. In all too many cases it has been taken for granted that the father of the child cannot be found or cannot help. It then falls to the state to provide for the children' (14 August 1995).

In this cameo, Redwood reiterated a point made after his visit to St Mellons housing estate in Cardiff two years earlier. He was then critical of 'the trend in some places for young women to have babies with no apparent intention of even trying marriage or a stable relationship with

---

4. There has been a well-recorded tendency for lesbians to be ignored by the legal and social, thus having the effect of rendering them invisible: Crane 1982; Beresford 1994; Boyd 1992; Laws 1994.

the father of the child' (*Daily Telegraph*, 3 July 1993). Other right-wing colleagues shared Redwood's concern about the financial burden placed upon the state by lone mothers. In 1992, at the Conservative Party Conference, Peter Lilley, then Secretary of State for Social Security, referred to his list of priorities for the following year. One of the groups that Lilley intended to target to make public expenditure cuts was lone mothers. In his speech he made reference to 'young ladies who get pregnant just to jump the housing queue' (cited in *The Observer*, 14 November 1993).

Both politicians alluded to the idea that young mothers have children in order to secure council housing. At the same time, the politicians were promulgating the notion of the wilful teenager who seeks to parent outside the boundaries of the marriage relationship. Moreover, these lone mothers were portrayed as draining public resources as a result of their dependency upon state benefits and public housing. The political condemnation of the lone mothers' perceived wilful and exploitative behaviour is reflective of the notion that children should have and need two parents and that women who elect to forgo the chance of providing a father for their children are being feckless and irresponsible. Redwood claimed that in many cases it is taken for granted by the women that the fathers could not or would not assist.

The above statements are indicative of a number of issues that preoccupied government ministers and party policy of the time. These include dependence upon state benefits, demands on public housing and a renunciation of men as fathers. Concerns such as the above were used to underscore claims made about the 'problem' of teenage lone mothers and their children. Many of the government's worries about lone mothers are financial, and policy and legislation such as the Child Support Acts attempted to fix financial responsibility on the non-residential father. Additionally, however, we find another example of the way in which these women are represented as expelling men from the familial realm. The teenage lone mother is constructed as making a conscious decision to go ahead and parent without the aid of the father. Given the strength of the idea that 'the family' as traditionally constituted is fundamental to society, it is not too difficult to see how the lone mother is represented as electing not to belong to society through the renunciation of men as fathers and thus also the foundational family form. As will be revealed in Chapters 3 and 4, the refusal to include a man in the child's life is rendered pathological by a number of influential discourses such as law, psychology and sociology. The teenage lone mother is moreover constructed as selfish, placing her own needs above those of her child and society. Lilley claimed that the motivation for pregnancy is to secure public housing.

According to the political rhetoric of the time, this is at the expense of the traditional family competing for limited resources. As Young writes:

> The parent who puts the child first (by not divorcing) is deemed to put society, the future and the government first. In other words, subjection to the child makes the mother a subject of society. Putting the child first is taken as evidence that the mother chooses to belong to society . . . Hence the selfish single parent can be made a symbolic outlaw, outside society.   (1996: 160)

Women's decision to go on and have children alone is clearly condemned by political discourse. Lone mothers who rely upon the state for support are represented as depriving the valorized two-parent family of valuable public commodities such as council housing. In so doing, they are regarding as posing both a moral and a financial threat to the traditional social order, which privileges 'the family'. Poor teenage lone mothers are seen as constituting part of an underclass removed from legitimate norms and mores governing the financially and morally responsible two-parent counterpart.

In 1993, John Gummer, then Environment Secretary, ordered an inquiry into alleged discrimination against two-parent families in allocating council housing. He was quoted as saying that as there was not 'all the accommodation in all the ranges in every place one would wish', it was necessary to set priorities and that 'families should come first' (*Daily Telegraph*, 5 July 1993). This statement is revealing of the way that lone mother headed households are not constructed as 'proper families'. Sir George Young, then housing minister, reiterated the priority of the two-parent family in October the same year. He asked: 'How do we explain to the young couple who want to wait for a home before they start a family that they cannot be re-housed ahead of the unmarried teenager expecting her first, probably unplanned child?' (*The Guardian*, 5 September 1995). The manner in which Gummer elected to set his priority as *families* coming first is indicative of how lone parent households headed by 'teenage' lone mothers are marginalized by many of the right-wing government discourses. According to his analysis, households headed by young lone mothers are not 'real' families. Moreover, Gummer is claiming that the 'teenage' lone mother's competing claim to local authority housing is depriving the laudable two-parent family, *the* family, of suitable living accommodation. The assumption of lone motherhood by young women is constituted as a drain on public resources. The government makes it clear that those who are defined as the most deserving of public housing are couples who conform to the norm of waiting to find a home before having children. In contrast, the teenage lone mother is portrayed as little more than a pariah with regard to her claim to public resources.

The association made between lone mothers and housing highlights the fact that there is a shortage of available public housing. This shortage, it is alleged, is due to the demand made by the increasing number of lone mothers who get pregnant to 'jump the housing list'. The alleged increase in the number of lone mothers has been exploded as a myth. As the statistics demonstrate, there has been a fall in the number of births to teenage mothers over the past twenty years. In 1993, Ann Holmes, director of the National Housing and Town Planning Council, maintained that the vast majority of young mothers live with their parents (*The Guardian*, 29 October 1993). Sue Slipman, former director of the NCOPF, stated that council housing is not automatically available to young mothers, because people under the age of eighteen are not legally able to hold a tenancy. 'Of those who do not stay at home, most go into mother and baby hostels or temporary bed and breakfast accommodation before getting a flat on their own' (*The Independent*, 6 July 1993). Claims that young lone mothers are given priority over two-parent families can therefore be questioned. Notwithstanding the mythical nature of the assertions made by Conservative government ministers in the 1990s, the idea of the 'feckless' teenager found its way into public consciousness. The potency of the imagery of the scavenging teenage mother was enhanced by the Conservative government's protracted political will to solve the 'problem' of young women having children alone. For by suggesting concrete solutions to what was perceived as a growing problem, the government at the same time reinforced the much-vaunted perception of seriousness. The suggestions were usually aimed at deterrence.

A number of schemes were put forward by the then government in an attempt to deter young women from having children alone. In 1993, it came to light that the Conservatives were considering capping benefits for any second and subsequent children born to lone mothers in receipt of state benefits. The scheme followed a similar model established in the American state of New Jersey. Michael Howard, the proponent of the changes, stated that the reforms would not be aimed at existing families but rather at *potential* parents who relied upon state benefits. The government, he stated, could ensure that a framework of 'incentives and disincentives' existed to encourage responsible behaviour (*Daily Telegraph*, 6 October 1993). Howard also revealed that there might be a possibility of reforms to make the adoption of children born outside marriage easier. He claimed that successive studies had indicated that the degree of commitment of parents has a 'critical impact on the extent to which children grow up as well-adjusted citizens' (*The Guardian*, 6 October 1993). The most committed parents, he opined, are adoptive parents. Married parents living together are the next most committed, with the least committed being unmarried parents not living together. At the same time, he claimed that studies had also shown that father absence can be deleterious for the child in that it can damage a child's educational achievement and foster criminality (see further, Wallbank 1997). Here, I am not concerned with discussing the validity of the research findings, though it would be interesting to examine the criteria used in establishing parental commitment levels. Rather, my concern lies in showing how Howard opted for a hierarchization of families that locates the lone mother headed household at the very bottom of the pile. At the same time, Howard alluded to the idea that father 'absence' is a destructive force in a child's life. The effect is that women who produce children with the intention of having no stable relationship are constructed as partaking in potentially destructive behaviour. They also often fail to attain the celebrated norms of self-sufficiency and independence. Lone mothers and particularly poor lone mothers are subjected to public scrutiny and placed under some form of state supervision. In relation to child support, women are not allowed to retain control over the decision as to whether to claim maintenance from the father of the child (see Chapter 1). Divorced women cannot be secure in decisions over paternal contact when they have strong reservations about the wisdom of contact and when that contact is under dispute (see Chapter 3). Fineman provides a useful (though not entirely unproblematic) distinction between the 'private' and 'public' family. She states: 'The public nature of the perceived inadequacies of single mothers justifies their regulation, supervision and control. "Private" families, by contrast, are protected. They exemplify the "natural" form and fulfill the natural function of families' (1995: 190–1). Lone mothers who are forced to rely on the state for support are represented as doing so at the cost to competing claimants who may be regarded as more deserving. However, Fineman neglects the way the two-parent family may also have to rely on the state for support and thus may be treated as 'public' families in need of a degree of supervision. Also, the lauded self-reliant family is subjected to state supervision through services such as health visiting. However, where Fineman's distinction works best is in the manner that lone mother headed families are rendered distinct for the ways in which they are perceived as lacking in both a private and a public sense. Lone mothers as against partnered ones are seen as potentially threatening to the child's well-being and also to the future of society. Lone mothers are rendered potentially destructive to the very foundation of society, and stringent supervision of lone mothers through law and public policy is justified on this basis. In other words, lone mothers are brought into the public arena by discourses rendering them distinct and defective in an economic and moral sense. They are therefore subjected to public supervision *specifically* because of their status as lone mothers.

The representation of lone mothers as destructive contrasts starkly with the popular notions of motherhood as productive. The productivity associated with motherhood as a social practice has long referred to the capacity of women to produce new and active members of society. It has also been increasingly argued that productivity refers to the provision of a commodity with exchange value in the market economy and the occasional political value in the contribution made in the fighting of a country's wars. Donzelot (1980) offers a historical perspective of how social practices such as infanticide, coupled with the high mortality rate in eighteenth-century France, came to be seen as a bad thing as there was at the relevant time a need for soldiers to fight in the country's wars. As such, the child came to be regarded as a product that had value to the state for the purposes of war or colonization. Katz Rothman offers a contemporary example of how a productive connotation is attributed to motherhood in the context of new reproductive technology. She argues that in this context mothers' work and mothers' bodies are resources out of which babies are produced. However, she stresses that according to the market not all work is of equal value, as is also the case with the value of the product (Katz Rothman 1994: 149).

This metaphor is useful in relation to the manner in which some groups of lone mothers are assigned less value than others. It is also of help in untangling the ways in which political discourse associates lone motherhood with the creation and continuation of what has been termed the 'underclass'. This is a theme discussed at length in Chapter 4 when I discuss non-residential fathers. However, it is useful to state the relevance of Charles Murray's underclass thesis for the discussion on lone mothers. His thesis contains the following message:

> It is becoming increasingly clear to all but the most blinkered of social scientists that the disintegration of the nuclear family is the principal source of so much social unrest and misery. The creation of an urban underclass, on the margins of society, but doing great damage to itself and the rest of us, is directly linked to the rapid rise in illegitimacy.
>
> (editorial, *The Sunday Times*, 28 February 1993)

According to Murray, the woman who chooses to parent without a man contributes to the annihilation of 'the family'. Illegitimacy is conjoined with the creation and perpetuation of the 'underclass'. Lone mothers are therefore held responsible for damage to their own families and to future families. There is an underlying assumption by Murray that lone mother headed families breed new ones, based on the idea that boys without good male role models will grow up into irresponsible fathers as they will know nothing else (see Chapter 4 for a more detailed analysis). The potential influence of lone mothers is therefore regarded as extensive, having the power to affect not only the present generation but also future generations. Finally, Murray's thesis pertains to the way many popular discourses of the 1990s polarized the lone parent family against 'the rest of us'. 'The rest of us' is interpreted as a means of setting lone mothers (constituting the underclass) apart from 'us'. This 'us and them' device reinforces the idea of belonging and unbelonging. Those who read and identify as 'us' constitute mainstream society. Lone mothers are represented as 'them', 'them' being outside or marginal to that society. They do not belong.

Lone mothers who wilfully exclude fathers from their children's lives are portrayed as marginal figures and unfit mothers. Their perceived unwillingness to form stable relationships with the fathers of their children is purported to be the cause of personal and social decay. As a result, the productive work of lone mothers is undermined and unvalued. What is worse is that lone mothers are represented as leeches who, rather than contributing to the well-being of their children and society, are instead responsible for sucking available public resources dry and cutting down their children's life chances. The Conservative government's focus was clearly upon reducing the numbers of young women who are constructed as wilfully assuming motherhood without a stable relationship.

In summary, the analysis of the Conservative government's targeting of 'teenage' mothers demonstrates that the problem of lone motherhood was constructed as concerning women who deliberately renounce the sanctity of the state-legitimated heterosexual relationship. While young lone mothers were not rejecting heterosex *per se*, they were, it is said, rejecting men as fathers. Young mothers were constructed as embracing the heterosexual act all too willingly. According to Conservative government ministers in the nineties, the purpose of lone mothers' pregnancy and mothering was ultimately to secure for themselves public housing and state benefits. The never-married mother was constituted as particularly threatening because of her perceived willingness to participate in heterosexual relations with men who were unlikely to fulfil their paternal responsibilities. In other words, the young mother becomes defined by her sexual encounters with irresponsible men/boys. Her sexual act is constituted as selfish and exploitative and includes the deliberate dissociation from boys/men as potential fathers. Moreover, a link is established between women's procreative capacity and the social and economic well-being of families in particular and society more generally. The lone mother's family is placed in competition for public resources against the valorized two-parent family. Conservative politicians sought to deprive lone mothers of public support on the basis that their families are not 'real' families. The characterization of the lone mother as a feckless teenager has had the potent effect of contributing to an undermining of an opportunity for female solidarity in campaigns to bring about reforms of the Act that would potentially benefit lone mothers who are in receipt of income support. Although the statistics show that the number of teenage pregnancies is in decline, the stereotype of the teenage mother as a social security scrounger is so potent that other lone mothers are keen to dissociate themselves from it. One of the most important effects of these negative representations is to divide women who are in receipt of state benefits into deserving and undeserving welfare beneficiaries. Lone mothers who have come into lone motherhood by the route of widowhood, the breakdown of a marriage or longstanding cohabiting relationship can and do on occasion dissociate themselves from the negative stereotype of the teenage mother.

It is understandable that this is the case, as women seek to constitute their own subjectivities in response to the negative representations that are made of them in discourses about lone motherhood. My point here, however, is that feminists, the Labour government and those who campaign on behalf of lone mothers should think carefully through the implications of making the distinction between the widowed, separated and divorced on the one hand, and the never-married younger mother on the other. There is a danger of falling into the trap of saying that younger mothers, unlike their older, divorced counterparts, are not deserving of public support. Lone mothers frequently take on board the stigma associated with being *reliant upon* state benefits, and this contributes to their low self-esteem at both a personal and a social level (see further, Chapter 5). It has been demonstrated in this section how the Conservative government used potent and devastating imagery about young lone mothers in order to warn of the potential for the destruction of the family and society. 'A woman and her children "alone" are considered an *incomplete*, and thus a deviant unit. They are identified as a source of pathology, the generators of problems such as poverty and crime' (Fineman 1992: 664).

Summary

In this chapter, I have highlighted how social and legal discourses differentiate the treatment meted out to lone mothers on the basis of their construction as either deserving or undeserving of reasonable legal and social support. In the first section, it was demonstrated that the law responds to women who are constructed as renouncing the norm of heterosexuality by rendering their families as outside the socially acceptable and legally endorsed family form. The legislation governing new reproductive technology denies women access to licensed treatment if they are unable to provide the child with a father or some other person who will be able to care and provide financially for the child in the absence of the carrying mother. Moreover, it has been demonstrated that by so doing the governing legislation valorizes and privileges the traditional family form over any other. Artificial insemination is perceived as a potential disruption to the social fabric on the basis that it destroys the need for the traditional two-parent family, which is regarded as the mainstay of society. As a result, the 'alternative' family form is marginalized.

I have also demonstrated how women who are regarded as overzealous in their embracing of heterosexuality are also seen as dangerous, though for reasons that contrast with the renouncing of the penile economy. The teenage mother is constructed as sexually over-active and wilfully so. She has too much male attention but without the relevant male having the corresponding financial responsibility. She is, therefore, reliant upon the state for support. This was problematic for the Conservative government as it sought to relieve itself of the financial responsibility for lone mothers and their children. Moreover, according to some contemporary academic and political discourses, it is still believed that children are being best served by two, preferably heterosexual, parents.

There is currently much renewed debate over the future of the family in political, legal, academic and popular discourse, with the emphasis often being upon identifying the cause of the decline in the traditional nuclear family. Legal debate has also focused upon providing solutions to the decline of 'the family', as has been the case with recent debates over divorce reform. Frequently, the debates posit the notion that if society could resurrect *the* family then other problems such as crime and delinquency would also be solved.[5] The effects for women who seek to parent alone are clear. They are discouraged from embarking upon such a course in the first place. The Conservative government's response to the constituted demon lone mother contained aspects of deterrence. For example, suggestions were made that lone mothers should no longer receive priority in housing policy. The myth that lone mothers receive priority in housing policy and practice has been exposed by lone parents' support groups such as the NCOPF. The Housing Act 1985 required local authorities to house priority-need homeless households, including pregnant women and people with dependent children. However, fewer than one in seven homeless households allocated dwellings in 1993 were for reasons of pregnancy (see further, Ford and Millar 1998: 16). Nevertheless, the Conservative government introduced the Housing Act 1996, which is intended to create a single route into public housing through the housing register (s.162). It was a move by the Conservative government to eradicate the mythical privileging of lone mother headed families. There is a body of evidence to suggest that in the context of lone motherhood there was under the Conservative government a political will to cut down women's reproductive choices.

It remains to be seen how the Labour government will proceed in relation to developing policy on lone motherhood. To date, the emphasis would appear to be on encouraging women's financial independence through paid employment, by ensuring men's parental responsibility for children and upon providing support for marriage. Even the most contemporary debates about lone motherhood and child support make it clear that there is strong support for the view that mothers should ensure as far as possible that a man contributes at least financially to his children's lives. In June 1997, Harriet Harman, Secretary of State for Social Security, announced the need for thorough review of the Child Support Agency due to the lack of fathers contributing maintenance (*The Guardian*, 9 June 1997). In 1999, the government published its White Paper on child support reform, as discussed in Chapter 1. The government makes a commitment to

---

5. On 31 October 1995, the BBC screened a programme made by Melanie Phillips called 'Who Killed the Family?'. One of the main arguments of the programme was that liberal intellectuals were responsible for the death of the family because of the promulgation of ideas such as it being acceptable for women to leave their familial responsibilities for the sake of their own personal fulfilment. See also Dennis and Erdos (1992), who argue that the problems of society could be solved if men were to return to their familial responsibilities.

ensuring that fathers who pay nothing will be treated harshly. Reforms include stricter enforcement methods and criminal sanctions for supplying false or misleading information to the Child Support Agency (White Paper 1999: 8 of 8). The Child Support Act is particularly concerned with enforcing a financial link between the child and her/his father. It is worth reiterating that one of the present government's main concerns about lone motherhood, as with the preceding Cabinet, is the financial burden of support. However, it has been shown that social and legal discourses are also concerned with maintaining the heterosexual relation, and right-wing political discourse has in the past constructed the taxpaying traditional family as more deserving of state support than the 'deviant' lone parent family. Moreover, a dominant motif that has inhered in and linked the social and legal representations of lone mothers is that some groups of mothers are more deserving of support than are others. Women who are constituted as wilfully rejecting the father and all the traditional trappings associated with that status are represented in both social and legal discourses in a derogatory manner. The current legal frameworks governing child support and new reproductive technologies serve to render wilful women who are determined to parent without men impotent. This book stands to remind the new Labour government that what women who parent alone need is empowerment and not denigration and hierarchization based upon the measure of the traditional two-parent family form. New Labour should stand as a metaphor for new ways of tackling important social and legal issues concerning the promotion of all family forms.

chapter 3

Mother knows best? Not in this court

In this chapter, I consider how the law constructs women when contact between non-residential fathers and children is disputed between the estranged partners. I examine the ways in which five Court of Appeal cases in the 1990s decided disputes over paternal contact and elucidate the criteria used by judges reaching decisions as to whether or not fathers should have contact with their children. I also unearth the significance of discourses that state that the interests of the child are best served through sustained contact with both parents. It will become clear that judges explicitly frame their decisions according to the best interests of the child and the welfare principle (Children Act 1989, section 1(1)). However, I argue that the concept is so vague as to give rise to the consideration of a number of influential factors that will affect the outcome to the detriment of the child and her/his mother. King is instructive here, as he argues that the welfare principle provides the symbolic function of legitimizing court decisions rather than prescribing a particular action and providing an outcome in an individual case. Rather, he claims the principle is used to form sets of 'harder-edged notions which can appear to offer a foundation for consistent decision making' (King 1987, cited in Davis and Pearce 1999: 144). In relation to disputed contact cases, the court begins with a number of strong suppositions about what serves the child's welfare. The notions that consistently appear in the case law are identified as:

1.　The implacable hostility of the mother.

2.　The desirability of father/child contact.

3.　The prominence of fathers' rights claims.

I also suggest that in taking account of the above factors, other important factors such as conjugal violence are ignored to the detriment of mothers and their children. Moreover, I demonstrate that mothers are subjected to vehement judicial disapproval for their resistance to paternal contact. My suggestion is that judges deny the possibility that mothers may know what is best for their children on the basis of their experience in providing day-to-day care. I also argue that the judicial disapprobation of mothers who are resistant to contact serves to bolster the idea that ongoing paternal contact is a laudable aim worthy of legal support. The final section outlines some suggested reform proposals and pinpoints a way forward for the developing law on contact.

The practical and emotional impact of such judgements on women is potentially far-reaching. Mothers are sometimes pathologized as deluding themselves to be acting in the best interests of their children. As a result, doubt is cast on the mother's ability to make rational decisions about her family's future. Furthermore, when judges latch onto the idea of the mother's hostility to contact it takes precedence over and negates the mother's reasons for wanting to frustrate contact between a father and his child. This may be the case even when there is strong evidence to suggest that paternal contact might not be in the child's best interests.

The moment of constructing women as 'implacably hostile' to contact serves to undermine her case for denial. In other words, in reaching a decision based upon the criterion of the best interests of the child, the so-called implacable hostility of the mother is rendered one of the most prominent factors influencing the outcome. The cases examined seem to spend a disproportionate amount of time considering the mother's attitude rather than the merits of her reasons for denial. At the same time, there is little judicial recognition of the possibility that mothers might know what is best for the children. Additionally, I posit that the idea that paternal contact is a laudable aim is assigned greater value by the courts than the everyday caring practices that mothers undertake for their children.

The judicial response

Many authors have demonstrated how judges and other legal actors have constructed mothers in a negative light when they are perceived as putting their own interests above those of their children. In the area of custody, it has been shown that when mothers deviate in some way from the idealized normative white, heterosexual, middle-class, traditional family form, they will at least be subjected to judicial disapproval and at most be deprived of the custody of their child. Behaviour that has been deemed to be worthy of negative construction has included lesbianism, adultery and placing great importance upon a career outside the home (Arnup 1989; Brophy 1985; Graycar 1989, respectively).

In this chapter, I elucidate the ways in which mothers who refuse to uphold contact orders are constructed as depriving their children of valuable contact with their fathers. I do not evaluate the competing merits of the parental claims in these cases. However, it is sometimes necessary to demonstrate how a mother's claim to know what is best for her children is overridden by the presumption that contact with the non-resident parent is in the best interests of children, frequently with scant regard for the substance of the woman's grounds for refusal. In the process of resolution, women who are constructed as wilfully depriving their children of the right to contact with their fathers are subjected to the court's frequently vehement disapproval. In some cases, a mother's refusal will prompt the threat of a punitive sanction, which may take the form of the judge threatening to make an order of costs (Re R (Contact: Consent Order) [1995] 1 FLR).

The undermining or negation of mothers' claims to know what is best for their children might be explained in part by the low value ascribed to the emotional care that women provide for their children. Here I adopt the notion of 'caring for' as formulated by Tronto, where the important distinction is made between 'caring for' and 'caring about'. 'Caring for' children is what mothers are usually involved in. Central to the concept of caring for is that care is a practical activity that involves an association between cognitive input and action (Tronto 1993: 108–9). 'Caring about', she suggests, has received more attention and more status with moral philosophers and reflects care in the more general sense of a *recognition* that care might be needed. It does not necessarily follow that the person who purports to care about someone or thing will go on to fulfil that identified care role. Caring for, on the other hand, will incorporate both aspects. Tronto argues that the practice of caring for has been left out of debates on morality. She advocates that caring for should be regarded as a moral practice and as such that it should not be marginalized in moral debates. At the same time, she argues that caring for should be accorded some considerable value, as care is a central concern of human life. Judicial pronouncement subjugates the mother's work of 'caring for' her child, in both an emotional and a physical sense, to the 'higher' abstract ideal of ensuring ongoing paternal contact.

The legal framework for decisions

The contact order is an order that requires the person with whom a child resides to allow the child to visit or stay with the person named in the order, or for that person and the child otherwise to have contact with each other (Children Act 1989, section 8(1)). There has been some confusion as to whether contact is the right of the parent or the child. While it is generally accepted that contact with parents is a fundamental right of the child, there has been a continuing controversy as to whether contact may also legitimately be regarded as a right of parents (McCall-Smith 1990: 10). While confusion remains about whether the father has a right to contact with his child, it will be posited that the ideology of a father's right to contact is currently so potent that the courts are reluctant to reject it. Concomitantly, the latter-day prominence of fathers' rights appeals also affects judicial decisions in contested contact cases.

The cases examined herein would seem to indicate that the courts determine the outcome on the basis of the welfare principle as laid down by the Children Act 1989, so justification for the decision would appear to be guided by the children's best interests as interpreted by the courts.[1] Thus, notwithstanding that contact is regarded as a fundamental right of a child, it is a qualified right that is subject to the welfare principle and the court's power of intervention. The concepts of welfare and best interests are 'notoriously indeterminate concepts', to such an extent that the crucial issue is not the concepts themselves but rather the choice of the decision maker (Mnookin 1975: 226; Bainham and Cretney 1993: 43). This chapter considers five cases. It seeks to examine the discursive processes of judgement faced by women who are constructed as being hostile to contact. To use a pertinent example, it has been posited that children suffer psychological damage as a result of a lack of paternal contact. This discursive statement, generated by a psychological framework, effectively lays down a scientific claim to know that the child who suffers paternal deprivation may turn out to be a damaged individual. The postulation that harm will be suffered by the child through paternal lack effectively places the

---

1. Section 1(1) of the Children Act provides:
    When a court determines any question with respect to:
    (a) the upbringing of a child, or
    (b) the administration of a child's property or the application of any income arising from it, the child's welfare shall be the court's paramount consideration.

child and her or his family in the network of power generated by that discourse as the family is constructed as a site of potential problems.

As established in Chapter 1, discourse therefore establishes a set of rules that may or may not be adhered to by individuals. Families may or may not choose to ensure ongoing paternal contact, but in the event that the child is constructed as damaged in some way the family that does not ensure paternal contact will be seen as falling outside the normative framework laid down by the psychological discourse. The family may then be treated as in need of some form of psychological or social modification. When called upon through some legal dispute, the law in particular will use extreme measures to modify the family and sustain the father/child relationship.

The presumption in favour of contact and against paternal deprivation is so strong as to prevent one mother gaining permission to emigrate (Tyler *v.* Tyler [1989] 2 FLR 158). It has recently been suggested that conflict and refusal of contact are constructed as the main dangers to the children of separating parents (Kaganas 1999). Contact between the father and child is not just seen as conferring some positive benefit to the child; a denial of contact is regarded as deleterious to the child's welfare. However, the extent to which contact 'in itself' has significance for the child's well-being has been questioned by Maclean and Eekelaar (1987, cited in Davis and Pearce 1999: 144–5). They argue, on the basis of North American studies over a twenty-year period, that the main issue affecting children is communication between parents and their 'interest in and closeness to the children' (cited in *ibid.*: 145). If we accept Maclean and Eekelaar's position, the important issue is not necessarily the contact itself but rather the quality of the relationships between the relevant parties. Despite this useful distinction, courts have often relied on the presumption that contact between father and child is desirable even when the facts establish good reasons for denying it.

Due to my narrow focus on a small number of cases concerned with the issue of paternal contact, my account of these cases is therefore and inevitably a partial one. It is partial in the sense that I look at a small number of cases, and my analysis does not seek any quantitative validation. The account is concerned to show the oppressiveness of the judicial responses in the case studies of Court of Appeal cases. While recognizing that appeal cases constitute only a minority of decided cases, they carry a great significance in terms of laying down the criteria by which future cases may be decided in the lower courts. Due to the doctrine of precedent, judges and magistrates hearing applications for contact are bound by the guidelines laid down by the Court of Appeal. My reading of the case law is also partial in the sense that I read and write the case studies as a feminist. Thus, I argue that it is politically expedient to unearth how mothers in similar situations are likely to be responded to by the courts so that women and their legal representatives might be more informed about the potential judicial response. Additionally, given the Lord Chancellor's current interest in contact and violence, the analysis highlights some of the problems arising from case law in this area (Advisory Board on Family Law: Children Act Sub-Committee 1999).

It will be shown in the analysis of these cases that mothers who contest contact between fathers and their children are portrayed negatively even in instances where they can demonstrate that either they, their children or both have been subjected to reprehensible behaviour by the child's father. Moreover, it will be shown that women who wilfully refuse continuing contact between children and their fathers are constructed as acting selfishly. There is a concomitant undermining of the notion that women know what is best for their children. A woman who is subjected to abhorrent behaviour by her estranged partner may well believe that he is likely to have an undesirable influence upon her children. She may have left the man in order to release herself and her children from these negative effects in the first place. However, women who refuse contact are at the same time represented as 'deluding' themselves into thinking that they seek to ban contact in the best interests of the child. Women are therefore pathologized as they are regarded as acting in an irrational manner about the issue of continuing contact. O'Donovan is instructive here:

> Femininity is constructed in legal discourse around the family as tenderness and warmth with children, as economic dependence on men, as physical need of protection . . . Women who do not fit easily into a construction of feminine frailty, whether because of the way they live or because of their rejection of this constructed role, are condemned.
> (1993: 75)

Women who wilfully resist paternal contact are constructed as renouncing the 'normal' feminine traits of tenderness, softness and frailty. Moreover, they are constructed as actively campaigning to keep the child from the father for their own selfish motivations. This has led to academic commentary seeking to deal with the problem of 'selfish' mothers who attempt to 'alienate' fathers from children (see further, Ingman 1996: 617; Maidment 1998: 264–5; and also Chapter 4, which deals with the concept of parental alienation syndrome). Women who resist contact are also attempting to get away from being emotionally and economically dependent upon men. In other words, they are represented as attempting to secure maternal autonomy in a socio-political climate that valorizes the traditional nuclear family. Their betrayal of the social order is therefore twofold.

I also reveal how judges sometimes override the advice of the welfare professionals who are involved with the cases. By so doing, legal agents are establishing a hierarchical claim to power that situates the discourses of the law in a prominent position of authority (Smart 1989: 17). Furthermore, the law has the opportunity to translate relevant scientific research findings to 'emerge in law as simple rules of thumb or normative dictates to parents' (King and Piper 1990: 126, cited in Davis and Pearce 1999: 144). In resolving legal disputes over contact, the law has a wide range of resources available to it, including discourses from the welfare professionals with a duty to the court and those from the academy. Psychological discourse lauds the continuation of contact, and the law elects to incorporate this into the umbrella concept of 'the best interests of the child'. It therefore becomes a legal rule of thumb that paternal contact best serves the child's welfare. Reece has argued that the 'indeterminacy of children's welfare has allowed other principles and policies to exert an influence from behind the smokescreen of the paramountcy principle (1996: 295–6). The breadth of the welfare principle allows courts to use specific principles in particular contexts. In this context, the presumption of contact is used to prescribe that women should ensure that paternal contact is ongoing. The basis of the mother's claim to knowledge about her children's welfare is frequently marginalized, undermined and sometimes disbelieved by the adjudicating courts as a result of the strength of the principle of continuing paternal contact. The practical implications are that judges are extremely reluctant to deny fathers contact with their children. While it is the case that decisions are framed in terms of the best interests of the child, judicial statements would seem to support the view that fathers also have an interest in continuing contact with their children. Also, courts are keen to show disapproval of those mothers who are constructed as depriving both the father and the child of contact. There seems to be considerable judicial support for the idea that father participation is a laudable end deserving of legal recognition and support.

Right to contact: the case law

In the first of the cases to be discussed, the parents of the child were not married and had separated one year after the birth of their child. The mother was granted custody, with reasonable contact by the father, and an order was made granting the father parental rights and duties. Contact took place on a fortnightly basis until it stopped as a result of a conflict between the parents. The mother appealed against the contact order between the father and the child, aged five at the time of the appeal. (Re P (A Minor) (Contact) [1994] 2 FLR 374). The appeal was dismissed on the basis that it was in the child's best interests to continue with contact. In Booth J's summation, it was stated that: 'there were problems between the mother and father. There have been some incidents of quite considerable and wholly unjustifiable and reprehensible violence by the father against the mother' (p.375: para. F). It was reported that the mother had been unwilling to disclose her address to the father. However, contact had continued for another year until the father became angered by the mother's refusal to furnish him with her address and had then left for an extended holiday in America without informing the mother of his whereabouts.

The summation also reveals how the father had refused to pay his maintenance order of £200 per month despite having received a substantial redundancy payment from his employer. On his return from the USA, he visited the home of the mother's parents and was again abusive and verbally threatening to the mother and the maternal grandmother. The mother in this case is praised by Booth J for 'her great efforts, and successful efforts, to obtain a livelihood for herself and her son, and also to undergo a 2 year college course in social care' (p.376: para. B). The court is provided with details of the mother's mental heath, it being demonstrated that she suffered from depression and anxiety. A psychiatrist verified the woman's condition.

This case is atypical in that the court played down the pathologization of the mother, favouring instead the view that the mother was a 'stronger character' than the doctor had found (p.379: para. H). In other words, the mother was found by the court to be less mentally vulnerable than had been established by the psychiatrist who gave evidence of a perceived threat to her mental health should contact be ordered by the court. This point is reiterated many times in the judgement. Moreover, the court threw doubt upon the psychiatric evidence by stating that his evaluation was based solely upon the mother's version of events. There are a number of points that arise from this.

First, it becomes apparent that the court is substituting the finding of the expert giving evidence with its own finding. The court alluded to the partiality of the doctor's opinion. As such, the law is reasserting its domination over the issue in need of resolution, thus establishing itself as more adequately equipped than the psychiatric expert to deal with dispute resolution in an impartial manner. Second, the court would appear to cast doubt upon the assertion of the woman's vulnerability. By so doing, her case for frustrating contact is undermined. The mother is constructed as a 'coper'.[2] The court thus rejects the risk to her mental health should contact be ordered. At the same time, the court's opinion about the mother's mental capability contains the implicit message that she has deceived the doctor about the extent of her depression in order to get the doctor onside. The main body of the judicial pronouncement of this case is concerned with the condition of the mother's mental health. It might be argued that such an in-depth assessment of the mother's mental health was necessary on the grounds that she attempted to establish that her health would suffer if contact were to be enforced. However, the court did not examine to anything like the same extent the violent behaviour of the father or his attitude towards his paternal responsibility and the possibility of a link between his violence and her depression.

While the judge was disdainful of the man's violent behaviour towards the woman, little space was dedicated to it in the final decision, effectively minimizing the potential impact upon his filial relationship. Moreover, the sole reference that is made to what I will call the father's mental capacity is that the judges in the court of first instance found him 'immature, self-centred and very much concerned with his own image'. Notwithstanding, they came to the conclusion that 'he did intend to be a responsible father for the future and that he acknowledged his irresponsibility in the past' (p.377: para. B). Despite the absence of a detailed account of the father's mental capacity (it only had his own word for it), the court was able to find that he intended to be responsible in the future. While the mother went to the length of securing the opinion of an expert witness in order to support her case for frustrating contact, the father merely asserted that he intended to be a responsible father in the future. The judge seemed satisfied with his assertion, and the mother's appeal was dismissed with the effect of ordering supervised contact between the father and the child.

This begs the question as to why the judge seemed satisfied with such flimsy evidence of the father's intention to become a responsible father in the future. It is easy to argue that the court based its decision on the presumption that continuing contact is in the best interests of the child as it renders this point explicit in its concluding remarks (p.380). What I am concerned with here are the criteria adopted in making a decision as to what is and is not in a child's best interests. It is apparent from the

---

2. See p.377, paras. C and D, where the judge goes to great lengths to outline how well she copes with major aspects of her life.

case law analysed above that anyone who seeks to capsize the premise that continuing contact is in a child's best interests will have to establish a very strong case against the continuation of contact. In the above-cited case, it would appear that the father's violence against the mother is regarded as insufficient reason to end contact between the father and the child.

It may be the case that the idea of the desirability of paternal input is so pervasive and dominant that judges are reluctant to reject it. There is also room to argue that the trivialization of the violence against the mother reflects a more general judicial apathy towards violence against women. It is not difficult to present a case claiming trivialization when the physical space dedicated to discussion of the husband's violence is minimal, especially when set against the space dedicated to the analysis of the mother's mental capacity. This finding coincides with the recent research of Hester and Radford on violence, contact and the impact of the Children Act 1989 on mothers (1996: 90). Their important study confirms that on occasions contact was used as an opportunity to be violent to the estranged partner (*ibid.*: 9). Additionally, they show that often women in their sample who had been abused still did not oppose contact and even facilitated it (*ibid.*: 24–5). However, when women did oppose contact, welfare professionals and the courts defined the problem as the woman's hostility rather than the violence of the man (*ibid.*: 23–6). The study also establishes that when fathers are seeking contact with their children, their ability to care is not examined in the same detail as the mothers'.

In contrast to the manner in which male violence is downplayed in the above case, the mother contesting contact finds that her own mental capacity comes under greater scrutiny than that of the father.[3] A startling omission, however, is that no association is made between the mother's mental health and the violence perpetrated against her. Furthermore, the evidence that is presented in order to establish the mother's mental health problems is rejected on the basis that the judges are better placed to adjudicate the mother's mental health than is the psychiatrist. Booth J states of the first instance decision:

> The justices had plenty of opportunity to observe the mother in a very stressful situation indeed and to form the view that she coped very well. The justices also found as a fact, and clearly they had

---

3. The pathologization of women in the criminal legal system has been sub-jected to scrutiny by Hilary Allen (1987), who shows how women are like-lier to be referred for psychiatric treatment than are their male counterparts.

evidence on which to do so, that she was *implacable in her hostility* towards the father and determined at all costs to prevent contact between him and the child.   (pp.378–9: paras. H–A, my italics)

The judge in this case clearly refutes evidence that suggests that the mother would be unlikely to cope with the continuation of contact between the father and the child. The statement is revealing of the manner in which mothers are expected to cope. What is more, the judge goes to the extent of suggesting that the mother is far from vulnerable and posits instead that she is extremely strong in stressful situations. The judge's construction of the woman's strength is reflected in the way in which she draws attention to her implacable hostility to contact. Far from being susceptible to mental illness if contact is enforced, the woman is constituted and responded to as a wilful and resolute woman who is determined to keep her child from having contact with his father.

In another more recent case (Re O (Contact: Impositions of Conditions) [1995] 2 FLR 124), the mother of a two-year-old boy opposed contact between father and son. Her being unwilling to participate in contact gave rise to the court imposing conditions to a contact order that required the mother to have contact with the father against her wishes. In his summary of the facts of the case, Sir Thomas Bingham MR briefly mentions the breaching of a molestation order, for which the father received a sentence of twenty-one days imprisonment (para. A: 125). The violence perpetrated against the mother by her estranged partner after separation is given no further attention. The remainder of his judgement refers mainly to a discussion of the grounds upon which decisions about contact are made. It holds that the interests of the parents are relevant only where they affect the welfare of the child. There is no mention of a potential link between the mother's sense of security and the child's well-being. This seems ironic given the proliferation of normative discourses that conflate a mother's interests or needs with those of her children (see further, Chapter 5). Perhaps more importantly for the discussion here, it establishes that it is almost always in the interests of the child to have contact with the other parent. The intransigent mother has no right of veto over contact (para. E: 124). The mother expresses concern that the child is upset by the contact between the father and the child. The judge minimizes the mother's concern by alluding to the earlier judgement of Latey J in the case of Re H (Minors) (Access) [1992] 1 FLR 148. Here it is stated that:

> where the parents have separated and one has the care of the child, access by the other often results in some upset in the child. Those

upsets are usually minor and superficial. They are heavily outweighed
by the long term advantages to the child of keeping in touch with the
parent concerned.   (para. G: 128)

The case makes clear that a mother's hostility to contact will not in
itself be sufficient to stop the order for contact being made. Moreover, the
concept that paternal contact is beneficial to the child overrides other considerations in the majority of instances. What this ignores is the link between
conjugal violence and women's maternal role. Hester and Radford highlight the way that women's experience of violence is profoundly affected
by their work as mothers and carers (1996: 89). I would add that the violence also influences women's caring work as mothers. So, for example,
the experience of violence may be a factor in deciding that the relationship is at an end because of the deleterious effect of it on the children.
Given the importance placed on continuing contact by the judiciary, there
is little room for consideration of these extenuating and important factors.

The problem of conjugal violence was raised again in the case Re P
(Contact) (Supervision) [1996] 2 FLR 314. The case concerned an appeal
by the father against an order made initially for indirect contact only. The
parents had two children, both male, aged eight and five at the time of the
appeal. The mother was hostile to contact for a number of reasons but
not least because of the father's repeated violent behaviour towards her.
The relationship had ended after the father had attempted to strangle the
mother and threatened to kill the children. He received a twelve-month
prison sentence, six months of which was suspended. The father's appeal
was successful, and direct contact with supervision was ordered.

Medical evidence was offered on behalf of the mother, who had in
the past suffered from psychiatric illness and drug abuse. The doctor in
the case stated:

she not only has no signs of any psychiatric disorder but shows
indications of having matured into a sensible and caring person
whose views about the welfare of her children and in particular about
the likely impact of regular contact with [the father] should be taken
extremely seriously.   (para. C: 318)

The doctor's assessment of the mother incorporates some recognition
of the emotional and cognitive aspects of caring for children as described
by Tronto. Moreover, the court is urged to take the opinion of the mother
into account when reaching its decision about future contact. However,
when reaching the decision to allow direct contact, Wall J highlights that:
'It is almost always in the interests of a child whose parents are separated
that he or she should have contact with the parent with whom the child

is not living' (para. F: 328). It is reiterated across several paragraphs of the judgement that while the implacable hostility of the caring parent is a factor to be taken into consideration in the decision-making process it is not in itself sufficient to prevent contact (see particularly para. F: 329).

In deciding the case, the court gave much weight to the idea that children need to relate to both parents. The words of the court welfare officer are instructive and clearly influential to the outcome. She/he stated that it is better for the children to see the father in order to enable them to relate to a person and 'prevent fantasies' (para. H: 319). What is perhaps also relevant to the court is the fact that the mother was living with another woman in a lesbian relationship at the time of the hearing. The opinion of the court welfare officer was clearly influenced by psychological discourse that speaks of the importance of a child maintaining contact with the father in order to ensure proper psychological development. As I discuss in the next chapter, Bly has written that father absence causes a hole to appear 'in the son's psyche, a hole that fills with demons' (1990: 77–8). The father is found to be crucial to the healthy development of sons in particular, though since the 1970s psychological sex role theories have been demonstrated as flawed for failing to account for the significance and potential impact of culturally defined constructions of gender (Oakley: 1972). Foucault has also provided important insights into the increased significance of new pedagogical disciplines such as psychology, as was discussed in Chapter 1. His concept of normalization is also useful for considering the case law decisions.

This chapter makes use of Foucault in that it seeks to reveal and examine the ways in which the judiciary constructs mothers when they fail to conform to the norm of continuing paternal contact. It is also concerned with highlighting the complexity and diversity of the relationship between normalizing discourse and the coercive aspects of the rule of law as applied by the judiciary. In the closing section of the judgement, Wall J offers the mother a warning against keeping the children from their father:

> Whatever she does, these children will want to know their father as they grow up, and if she continues to obstruct contact she will . . . simply be storing up trouble for herself. If she impedes contact, one day the children will be old enough to see their father despite her wishes, and if they discover that he is not the monster she has painted, they will blame her for keeping them away from their father.
> (paras. B–C: 333)

This statement ignores the mother's rationale for wanting to keep the father from the children. The judge perceives the resistance to contact as a risk to the mother's own future relationship with her children. Given the mother's experience of extreme violence, it is not surprising that she might consider the risk well worth taking. It is much propounded by the judiciary that it is women's hostility that is the main problem in cases involving contact. However, as the research above indicates, women will generally try very hard to maintain contact and only attempt to restrict or prevent it if they feel the children's or their own safety is jeopardized (Hester and Radford 1996: 89).

The concept of implacable hostility arises time and again in cases where mothers are resistant to father/child contact. When the concept is brought into these cases, judges are keen to demonstrate a reluctance to 'allow the implacable hostility of one parent to deter them from making a contact order where they believed the child's welfare required it' (Re J (A Minor) (Contact) [1994] 1 FLR 729: para. G). It would appear that once judges have constructed a mother as implacably hostile to contact other considerations, such as the motivation for her determination to keep the father away from the child, are frequently ignored or trivialized, as in the above case. Notwithstanding, judges will refrain from making a contact order if they can demonstrate that they are acting in the child's best interests. However, in coming to a decision as to what is in the court's view the best interests of the child, judges will frequently pour scorn upon the mother who is constructed as determined to frustrate contact. They will at the same time fail to give due consideration to the mother's reasons for her obstinacy in the matter.

The concept of implacable hostility was discussed at length in the case of Re J (A Minor) (Contact) [1994] 1 FLR 729. In this case, the father was appealing against a decision of an earlier court not to make an order for contact. The court dismissed the father's appeal on the grounds that the original decision not to make an order was correct on the finding that to do so would cause the child harm. Despite this, the court was keen to stress that judges should be reluctant to allow the implacable hostility of one parent to deter them from making a contact order where they believed it to be necessary for the child's welfare. The case involved a boy aged ten whose parents were divorced. The mother was granted custody and the father was granted reasonable access, which was successful for a six-year period. The mother terminated contact after an incident in which the father smacked his son, aged eight at the time. The father made an application for contact to the court. The welfare officer reported that it was not in the child's best interests to be forced into a situation that was fraught with anxiety and insecurity. When the matter came before the court, it was decided that there would be no order for contact on the basis that stress would be caused to the child if contact were to be enforced. A major factor taken into consideration by the court was the mother's 'implacable hostility' towards contact.

The father in this case had initially, it was recorded by the welfare officer, been encouraged by the mother to have contact with the child. The mother, however, did stop access after an incident when the son had reported seeing a pornographic photograph. The parents discussed the matter, reassurances were given and access was resumed. The father also had a conviction for living off immoral earnings, and it was reported that the son, while with the father, was permitted to watch pornographic videos. This was another issue of contention between the parents. Additionally, the welfare officer also reported that the son had complained of being left for varying periods. The final incident that caused the complete cessation of contact was one in which the father smacked the son for not obeying an instruction. It was reported that the father had smacked his son, sworn at him and then hit him again (p.731: paras. C–H). According to the original judge, after hearing the welfare officer's evidence he came to the conclusion that 'the real cause of access coming to an end was the mother's feelings fuelled by her own mother and by her new husband, P. She had very strong adverse feelings against [the father]. He had in a sense, played into her hands, by his conviction'. Later, he stated that 'she believes very deeply that it is not in the child's interests to see his father'. Again later, the judge stated a finding that it would be beneficial for the child to have contact with his father, especially during the child's teenage years. However, the judge noted:

> My problem is that I do not believe that the mother sees this case in the way I see it. I believe she is a mile away from seeing it in the way that I see it. I do not believe she understands at the moment what I am saying about the benefit to the child of keeping in contact with the father.   (p.733: para. C)

In reaching his final decision, the appeal judge emphasized the original judge's construction of the mother's resistance to contact by quoting huge segments of his opinion, including the above. He continued:

> This is an unusual case because the mother's degree of hostility is about as great as I have ever come across. [And I remind myself that this is a very experienced judge in this field.] She is able to *deceive* herself into believing that the reason why access is not taking place is because the boy does not want it . . . I have come to the conclusion that she is a person who has no *rational* judgement of this whole situation of what is in C's best interests with regard to access . . . *I am*

satisfied that she would continue to be implacably opposed to it, that she would continue to communicate this to the boy and that he would be placed under considerable pressure.   (p.734: paras. C–G) (my italics)

One of the most striking features of the judge's opinion is the vitriolic nature of the attack against the mother in this case. The judge is severely critical of the way in which the mother's understanding of the issue of contact departs so radically from his own. Furthermore, he makes reference to the idea that the mother is incapable of understanding the potential benefits to the child of maintaining contact with the father. (This is a fact that can surely be questioned given the mother's initial willingness for contact.) Again, I am concerned here with how judges come to reach a decision as to what is in the best interests of the child. In other words, what criteria are adopted in reaching a decision that they can claim to be in the interests of the relevant child? In this case, the mother is castigated for her inability to think about the benefits of contact in the same way as the judge. Judicial attention is devoted to exposing what he believes is her mental incapacity for rational thought. Once more, the father's behaviour, although outlined in the judgement, is subjected to little scrutiny by the court, even though there is room to argue that for the mother this may have seemed 'cogent' enough reason to cease contact. I must reiterate, however, that I do not seek to assess the competing claims of parents in these cases but rather to examine the manner in which women who seek to frustrate contact are constructed by the judiciary.

I am not suggesting that all mothers act in the best interests of their children all of the time, but in this case there is evidence to suggest that the mother may have ceased contact believing that the father's influence would have a negative impact on her son. The only link that is made in the judicial pronouncement between the father's behaviour and the mother's hostility to contact is when the judge states that the father 'had, in a sense, played into her hands by his conviction' (para. A: 773). The father's behaviour is not subjected to scrutiny in anything like the same way as is the mother's purported hostility to contact. Her hostility is said to be great, and the judge is clearly condemnatory of the extent of her feeling. Furthermore, her hostility towards the issue of contact is constructed as rendering her incapable of rational judgement, so much so that she is perceived as deceiving herself into believing that the child does not want contact.

In the judge's opinion, she will continue to be implacably hostile to contact and will put pressure on her son. Here, the judge ascribes characteristics to the woman that are viewed in a negative light by agents of the law. The law is rational; therefore the mother is outside the law. She is perceived and constructed as acting in a manner that is against the legal principle that the child has a right to contact. She is therefore rejecting the law in favour of the view that she and not it knows what is best for her child. The law responds by castigating her and her rejection of the law. The judge goes so far as to say: 'No doubt every mother thinks that she knows her own child best, but the courts have, over the years, acquired considerable knowledge and experience in cases of this kind' (ibid.: 736). The judge claims that the courts and not the mother know what is in the best interests of her child. As a result, the years of the mother's caring work are marginalized, with the law raising its own experience in similar cases to a position of prominence. The mother in this case is constructed as incapable of rationality and as prone to delusions about what is in the best interests of her child. What is perhaps worse is that the mother is presented as acting in a manner that is deleterious for her son, for if she continues with her implacable hostility, then she will subject her child to pressure.

The caring aspect of mothering work is normally associated with the nurturing and physical and emotional support of children. By constructing the mother as implacably hostile, she is presented as the polar opposite of a loving and concerned mother. The woman in this case is constructed as being potentially destructive of her child's well-being. She is seen as contravening the most fundamental criterion of femininity – maternal love.

The vehemence of the judicial response to the mother indicates the strength of support for the principle of continuing contact between a child and his/her biological parent. It is otiose that a judge is bound by the welfare principle in this matter. Notwithstanding, it is also the case that in reaching a decision based upon the best interests of the child there is room to argue that a more balanced consideration of the reasons for a mother's hostility should be undertaken. In other words, there should be a fuller consideration of the reasons why women in these cases are so strongly opposed to contact and some account taken of the caring work that mothers do for their children.

It has been demonstrated, however, that the mother who is constructed as 'implacably hostile' to contact with the non-residential parent, usually a father, cannot always expect a sympathetic response from the courts. Judicial attention is overwhelmingly concerned with the mother's perceived determination to keep the child from the father. While the courts acknowledge that it is the right of the child to have contact with his father, it has also been claimed on occasion that the welfare of a child required the court to 'inflict injustice upon the parent with whom the child was not resident' (para. G: 729). This alludes to the idea that the father also has a 'right' to contact with his child (see further, Chapter 4). The mother is therefore constructed as depriving both parties of contact.

The final case to be examined concerns divorced parents and their son, aged four at the time of the hearing (Re W (A Minor) (Contact) [1994] 2 FLR 441). In this case, as in the preceding case, the mother had re-partnered. On re-partnering, it was alleged by the court, she made 'what appeared to be a conscious and deliberate decision to cease allowing the boy to have contact with his father. In March 1991 the mother terminated contact' (para. C: 441). The following year, the father applied to the court for contact to be defined. The mother opposed the application on the grounds that the father was incapable of caring for the child, that he had not seen him for a year and that he would not retain an interest in him. The court made an order for contact between the child and his paternal grandparents as a means of re-establishing contact between the father and the child. The mother stopped all contact with the grandparents and stated that the child was to be raised to believe that the stepfather was his real father.

The judge in the court of first instance relied upon the 'no order' presumption in the Children Act 1989 and refused to make a contact order, on the basis that it would cause harm and destabilizing unhappiness for the child.[4] The mother and stepfather indicated that they would go to prison rather than obey a contact order. The biological father appealed. The question of contact was identified as a continual source of problems. The parents had separated two months after the birth of the child. The mother returned to work and the child was originally cared for during the mother's working hours by the paternal grandparents. The father had what was then called 'access' to the child once a week, the child at the time being cared for by the mother with the assistance of a child minder. In 1991, the mother began working at weekends, and the paternal grandparents cared for the child. The same year, the mother met her new husband and then ended contact with the father. The Appeal Court judge notes that the original judge's opinion is twenty-two pages long and that in it the history of the issue of contact is considered. The appeal judge recalls what is said by the first instance judge about the father:

> Father, as I find is an open, warm-hearted, jovial and possibly – may I put it this way – a little immature. Mother, alas, is a very different

---

4. Section 1(5) states that where a court is considering making an order under the Children Act 1989, it must not 'make it unless it considers that doing so would be better for the child than making no order at all'.

type of personality; rather close, introverted, if I may put it that way, and she has more than usual difficulty in entertaining any kind of opinion unless it is her own and feels very hurt if any such opinion should, in any way be forced upon her, or if anybody should attempt to persuade her, contrary to her own opinion.　(paras. E–G: 443)

The Appeal Court judge acknowledges that the original judge had accepted the evidence of the father as to how matters had developed after the separation. It is also noted that the mother had made a number of criticisms of the father and of his character, all aspects of which the judge had rejected. However, he did later state:

I am quite satisfied that although he may not have been the most sensible of fathers, father, until March 1991, exercised full contact with R, that he loves R and that he brings these proceedings not, as mother has said, because he hates her and wants to hurt her, but because he genuinely loves R as any normal father does love his little boy.　(paras. H–A: 444–5)

The appeal case report reveals nothing about the nature of the criticisms that the mother makes of the father. In other words, the reader is not made privy to any of the substance of the mother's apprehensions about contact as once the judge has rejected her reasons for frustrating contact, they then need no further consideration. The judge's opinion about the father is short and contains sentiments with an endearing quality. He is 'open, warm-hearted, jovial'. On the other hand, the mother is 'alas' very different and the judge indicates that she is very opinionated. In the assessment of the characters of the mother and the father, the judge expresses what would appear to be an almost fond view of the father. The mother by contrast is portrayed as a wilful woman, a harridan-like figure, and irascible should anyone seek to disagree with her. Furthermore, the construction of the mother's wilful and opinionated manner is heralded as a source of sorrow for those coming into contact with her. This is evident in the judge's use of the interjection 'alas'. The mother's claims that the father wants to hurt her are also rejected, though we are never informed as to the basis and substance of the mother's concerns about contact. Later, the original judge is cited as stating:

I wish mother would understand that the only vibes of hatred in this case came from her, and those vibes will destroy her, destroy the marriage and destroy R, and it is for his sake I express the most earnest hope that she will try to reassess her approach to life generally and to this particular difficulty in particular.　(para. E)

Here, the judge launches a dire caveat against what is considered the mother's propensity for hatred. He maintains that her 'vibes of hatred' will destroy all those who come into contact with her. Her destructive powers are represented as being on a Medean scale. The Euripidean mythical sorceress murders her children when Jason abandons her. According to Marina Warner, her maternity is her terrain of authority, and she perverts her motherhood because her motherhood remains the principal ground of her power. Medea the child murderer contravenes the most fundamental criterion of femininity – maternal love (Warner 1994: 6–7). The judge wants to make the mother see the error of her ways before it is too late. The judgement is prescriptive, and the judge claims to know the situation better than the mother herself. In this case, as in the previous one, the mother is found to be 'deluding herself that she was acting in the best interests of' her child (p.443: para. H).

The mother is represented as incapable of knowing what is best for her child. She is depicted as a woman who deceives herself and tries to deceive others into believing that she is acting in her child's best interests. Again, the mother's mental capacity for rational thought is undermined. The main focus of the judicial pronouncement is upon the mother's incapacity to know best. The court castigates her for wilfully keeping her child from his biological father. Scant attention is paid to her own experiences as to what is in the best interests of her child. In this case, the father's appeal is upheld and contact is ordered.

It has been demonstrated that even when a decision is made in favour of the mother, if the woman in question is perceived as determined to keep the father from the child then she will be subjected to vehement judicial disapproval for her determination. In other words, if the lone mother is constructed as 'implacably hostile' to the idea of continuing contact with the biological father the judiciary will sanction her for her displays of wilfulness. It has been noted that when the biological father has been replaced by a responsible social father, providing an appropriate substitute traditional nuclear family, the importance of the biological father may well be diminished (Smart 1987: 98–117). However, in the light of contemporary legislative innovations, the importance of the biological father is amplified. For example, the introduction of the Child Support Act has reinforced the significance of biological fatherhood, so it would be wrong to suggest that there is either a social or a legislative trend towards supplanting the biological father with a social father, at least in respect of financial responsibility. Moreover, the gain in prominence of the idea that fathers have a right to contact with their children may be significant in the judge's perception of whether or not contact should be enforced.

Prospects for reform

In 1999, the Advisory Board on Family Law: Children Act Sub-Committee issued its consultation paper (*Contact Between Children and Violent Parents: The Question of Parental Contact in Cases where there is Domestic Violence*). The scope of the consultation exercise covers 'the problem of domestic violence involving, or in the presence of, children and its relevance to contact' (p.2). It responds to a 'powerful body of opinion' that the Children Act 1989 needs to be amended to introduce a presumption against contact where domestic violence has been established (p.4). The opinion referred to includes women's groups, academics and the Association of Chief Officers of Probation (ACOP). The consultation paper states the preliminary views of the advisory board and seeks comments on its initial suggestions. Its position at the time of writing is that the problem of conjugal violence can be addressed within the existing legal framework, accompanied by new guidelines for good practice. For a full account of the suggested guidelines, see the Advisory Board: pp.25–8.

Here, I will identify some of those aspects of the advisory board's proposed guidelines that are relevant to the above case law analysis and that are problematic. First, good practice guidelines do not have the same legal standing as statute and fail to make the same stamp on public consciousness as primary legislation. Thus, the message that conjugal violence will not be tolerated in any circumstances is a little thin. Second, and very much related to the above discussion about the existing legal framework, is the way that the guidelines appear to write the child's primary carer out of the story. The advisory board suggests that:

> In deciding the issue of contact the court should, in the light of the findings of fact which it has made, apply the individual items in the welfare checklist with reference to those findings; in particular, where relevant findings of domestic violence have been made, the court should in every case consider the harm which the child has suffered as a consequence of that violence and the harm which the child is at risk of suffering if an order for contact is made.   (*ibid.*: 27(2))

It is difficult to see how the above guidelines alter the existing position, as they merely reiterate the welfare principle enshrined in the Children Act 1989. The very most the guidelines do is to stress the importance of a consideration of the impact of the violence upon the welfare of the child. Under the current law, when violence has been established this should be one of the factors taken into consideration when reaching a decision. Additionally, later proposals suggest that the court should consider the effect of the domestic violence on the child and on the parent with whom the child is living (27(a)). This restates what is said at 27(2) and adds nothing regarding the child's position. However, we do see the introduction of concern with the parent with care (who will almost always be a woman). The real gap in these guidelines is a consideration of the important relationship between women and children's welfare and how often the well-being of either party is frequently contingent upon the other (see above, p.16). Moreover, the proposals fail to take the mother's view of the effects of the violence on her child(ren) into consideration at all. The suggested guidelines appear only to mimic and reiterate the problems with the existing legal framework. If the guidelines are taken up, then I can foresee no way in which these particular aspects enhance the current situation for women and children. There is no instruction about the importance of taking the primary carer's view of the potential harm to the child into consideration. Again, women's 'caring for' work is written out of the decision as to what might be best for the child. This is in stark contrast to the position in New Zealand legislation, which has implemented the presumption against contact in its relevant provisions.

Section 16B of the New Zealand Guardianship Act 1968 (as amended by the Guardianship Amendment Act 1995) is headed: *Allegations of violence made in custody or access proceedings, and applies to all contact applications*. Sub-sections 4 and 5 are directly comparable with the advisory board's suggested guidelines (noting that New Zealand's guidelines are statutory). Sub-section 4 pertains to the presumption against contact and states that the court will only make an order to the 'violent party' if it is satisfied that the child will be safe during 'custody' or 'access'. In considering the child's safety, the court should have regard to a number of matters. Most of these pertain to the violence, past and future. Importantly, however, (f) states:

> Whether the other party to the proceedings (i) considers that the child will be safe while the violent party has custody of, or access to, the child and (ii) consents to the violent party having custody or, or access to, the child.
>
> (cited in the advisory board's consultation paper *Contact Between Children and Violent Parents*: 49–50)

The 'other party to the proceedings' in England and Wales is likely to be the woman with primary care. The New Zealand legislation shows an understanding of the importance of the woman's role in assessing matters pertaining to her child(ren)'s welfare. The mother's assessment of the risk to her child is made a central feature in the court's decision. Furthermore, the court should have regard to whether or not the woman consents to the 'custody' or 'access' (note the comparable English terms are 'residence' and 'contact'). Here, an important distinction is made between the risk assessment and the consent issue. Women are actively encouraged to forward their views on the likely impact to the child's welfare and also to airing their views on the desirability of contact with the 'violent party'. In effect, women are actively encouraged to participate in the decision-making process under the New Zealand system, rather than being marginalized and castigated, as can be the case in the existing English system. It is also useful that the New Zealand approach shows disapproval of the person perpetrating the violence by naming the offender as 'the violent party'. Here, the legislation starts from the premise that the 'violent party' will be prevented from contact with the child. Therefore, the law contains the very clear message that the 'violent party' is undeserving of contact and also and crucially that violence is almost always potentially deleterious to the child's welfare. In constructing the legislation in this way, men who have been found to be violent are forced to try to show that they have their children's interests in mind in seeking contact. It is a useful counterpoint to the idea that merely attaining the status of father is sufficient to ensure contact with a child despite a history of violent behaviour. The New Zealand legislation has much more emphasis on protecting women and children from violence. Women are encouraged to participate actively in important aspects of the process, leaving less room for the development of legal concepts such as 'implacable hostility' that have been used in a pernicious manner against women in disputes over contact. Under the New Zealand approach, it seems likelier that courts will have an expectation that women who have experienced conjugal violence will be opposed to contact and, moreover, that that resistance to contact is reasonable in the circumstances. As a result, women are unlikely to be subjected to the degree of disapprobation that they have faced in English courts. Indeed, they may be treated with a good deal of sympathy and understanding. The advisory board's consultation paper recognizes the advantages of the New Zealand legislation, including the protection of women and children and the advancement of treatment programmes for offenders. The disadvantages are said to be the cost of perpetrator programmes, the need for primary legislation and a slow litigation process (*ibid.*: 52–3). It is clear to see that a government committed to solving the problem of conjugal violence would see reform of the current law on contact as a reasonably inexpensive measure if counted in terms of the security of women and children at risk from violent men. The present government may regard the cost of the wholesale adoption of the New Zealand system as prohibitive. There is no reason, however, why a start could not be made with instituting primary legislation that embodies the presumption against contact when the non-resident parent has been shown to be violent. This would send a clear message to society at large that violence against women and children will not be tolerated and is pernicious to children's welfare.

Summary

In this chapter, I have used the Foucauldian lens to examine the way that judges in the English jurisdiction construct and respond to women who seek to end contact between a child and her/his biological father. It is argued that women who are regarded as 'implacable' in their endeavours to end contact are subjected to stringent scrutiny by judges, with the emphasis being upon the mother's mental capacity to think, know and act in her child's best interests. The scrutiny of mothers occurs at the expense of a thorough consideration of her reasons for implacability. In other words, the judges' construction of a woman's wilfulness as a negative attribute is sufficient to dispense with the need to consider the reasons for her resistance. As such, once women's implacable hostility to contact can be established by the courts, all discussion about what is and is not in the child's best interests is framed in terms of the mother's hostility to contact. Furthermore, the judiciary is scornful of behaviour that is deemed destructive for the future relationships between her, her child and the child's father. The court adopts the normalizing discourses of psychology and sociology in order to justify enforcing paternal contact. When deemed necessary, the court will also use threatening and coercive means with which to chastise uncooperative mothers.

Additionally, as a result of the judicial propensity for focusing upon women's mental capacity, it is possible to conclude that judges have very low expectations of fathers in deciding whether or not contact will be in a child's best interests. These low expectations may arise as a result of the dominance of the idea that children need fathers and that contact is generally a good thing. They may also be explained to a degree by the rise in fathers' rights campaigns, which have sought to use the idea that courts have shown a tendency to favour the mother in decisions regarding the custody of children (Brophy 1985). Groups such as Families Need Fathers (FNF) and Dads After Divorce (DAD) assert that they are getting a raw deal as far as the way they are constructed in discourses about parenting generally and child support in particular (Wallbank 1997). Additionally, the attitudes against women who are perceived as wilfully keeping their children from men can be seen as stemming from a reaction against the successes of liberal feminism, which have rendered it more acceptable for women to parent alone.

The cases examined herein would seem to indicate the contrary position, that a woman, in order to show herself to be a fit mother before the courts, must acquiesce in keeping the child's father involved in their lives. Where women can be demonstrated to be 'implacably hostile' to contact between the biological father and the child, she may find herself subjected to an abhorrent degree of judicial disapprobation. Finally, in reaching a decision about contact based upon the criterion of the best interests of the child, the judicial focus upon the mother's mental capacity takes precedence over any other potential aspect of the case. The basis of the mother's apprehension about contact are to all intents and purposes marginalized or ignored, perhaps at the expense of the child's best interests. Some of the above concerns might be met by adopting the presumption against contact in cases involving violence. However, it would be naive to imagine that all the problems faced by women in relation to contact disputes could be resolved by the above-named reforms. There will inevitably be problems of definition in relation to what constitutes a sufficiently culpable act and degree of violence to warrant the prohibition of contact (see, for example, Radford 1996). Additionally, professionals involved in contact proceedings may have no awareness of the difficulties involved in obtaining women's disclosure of incidents of violence (Barnett 1999: 105). While it is important to reconsider the law on contact where violence is involved, there is also a need for courts to consider seriously other forms of behaviour that might not be defined as violent but that are potentially pernicious to the child. An example of this might be the circumstances in Re J above, where the child had been given access to pornographic material. However, the government's concern with the present system of the resolution of contact disputes is welcome. It is to be hoped that the reforms will be more radical than has been initially suggested by the advisory board.

chapter 4

Fathers as 'victims': mounting a challenge to mothers

In Chapter 2, I discussed the ways in which social and legal discourses rendered women constructed as renouncing men as fathers as problematic. Additionally, links were made between the disruption of the traditional nuclear family and the creation of Murray's 'underclass'. This book is ostensibly concerned with women as mothers. However, it is axiomatic that in the context of post-separation families one cannot talk about mothers without paying some attention to fathers in order to show how different power relations between women and men play within the relevant discourses. Chapter 2 raised the discussion about boys needing fathers as role models. This chapter develops this theme through an analysis of discourses surrounding the enactment of the Child Support Act in the early 1990s. It also reveals how powerful discourses from pertinent academic disciplines are used to posit a certain 'truth' about the importance of fathers for the security of 'the family' and for the well-being of children. Additionally, it demonstrates the class-based nature of the campaign against the Act and how middle-class non-residential fathers succeeded in establishing themselves as 'victims' of an over-zealous and interfering state.

The implementation of the Child Support Act and the first years of the operation of the Child Support Agency prompted vehement criticisms from many quarters. Perhaps some of the most implacable critics were middle-class non-residential fathers, who claimed that they were being treated unfairly by the new measures. Non-residential fathers were joined by their new partners to voice concerns about the way the Act placed a greater financial burden on the reconstituted family. Fathers maintained that they were being targeted by the Child Support Agency as the best means of recouping the greatest amount of money for the Treasury as they were already paying maintenance and were therefore readily identifiable for child support purposes. Non-residential fathers as a group also objected to the way in which they were represented in many contemporary discourses in a negative manner. Fathers were constructed as 'absent' in both the White Paper *Children Come First* (HMSO 1990), which preceded the legislation, and in the Act itself. In much of the press coverage on the child support issue, non-residential fathers were constructed as feckless and in derogation of their paternal responsibilities. It resulted in men being represented as 'Other' to 'the family'. (For an exposition on the relationship between men and the family in a criminological context, see Collier 1998. The term 'Other' is borrowed from p.96.) This derisory construction of fathers provided a springboard for non-residential fathers' campaigns for reform of the legislation. They suggested that the Child Support Agency was failing to target those fathers who had never paid maintenance and who were absent in both emotional and financial terms from their children's lives. In recognition of the inflammatory nature of the language used to define these men, I have elected to use the term 'non-residential father' as an alternative throughout this chapter.

Middle-class fathers rebelled against the way that they were constructed in discourses about child support as 'absent' or 'feckless', stating that these constructions were inaccurate and unjust. Moreover, non-residential fathers argued that the new measures were unfair in that they set the new level of maintenance at an unreasonably high level, with no account being taken of their newly assumed familial responsibilities. The campaigning middle-class father who was already contributing financially to his first family, thus allowing him to demonstrate some responsibility towards his children, sought to establish a distinction between himself and the 'feckless' father who was in complete derogation of his paternal duty.

The media frequently expressed unquestioning sympathetic support for the middle-class fathers and their new partners. As such, it is the middle-class father who is privileged in social and legal discourses, as is evidenced by the changes implemented as a result of the Social Security Committee's reports. As Chapter 1 demonstrated, the changes made to the Act and to the CSA's operation almost exclusively serve to benefit middle-class non-residential fathers and their new families directly. In effect, non-residential fathers who had re-partnered and assumed the responsibility of a new family were rewarded by legal changes providing a new allowance for the housing expenses incurred by the second family. This privileged legal position was partly attained by non-residential fathers successfully establishing distance between the 'feckless' father of contemporary folklore and the active, participating father who just happened not to reside with his biological children. In other words, middle-class fathers sought to construct themselves as non-residential fathers who remained responsible for and responsive to their children's needs. They then wanted to distinguish their constructed subject position from that of the demonized feckless father, who is represented in contemporary debates on child support as lacking in all aspects of paternal responsibility. This is the matter to which I now turn.

Fathers *in absentia*: not guilty?

In defining the 'problem' of child support, the Conservative government at the same time constructed a normative framework against which parental behaviour was to be measured and adjudicated. The Child Support Act sets down a minimum acceptable standard of parental behaviour in the post-separation or divorce context. It is clear that the Act is predominantly concerned with ensuring that fathers continue to maintain their children financially. Additionally, the notion of ongoing parental responsibility at the centre of the Act serves as a legislative restatement of the paternal 'duties of kinship which are not negotiable' (Neale and Smart 1995: 38). These duties of kinship include the father having regular contact with the child. While it is difficult, if not impossible (let alone always desirable), to ensure that fathers retain contact with their children in the post-separation context, the Child Support Act offers a financial incentive to fathers to retain regular contact with their biological children.[1] It becomes possible to argue, therefore, that despite the primacy given to the financial nexus between the father and his children in the legislation, the Act also places some importance upon the idea that paternal contact is desirable and should be rewarded as such.

The question that then becomes important is how the law arrives at the idea that paternal contact is beneficial to children. The answers were hinted at in the last chapter. When addressing this matter, it is necessary to consider the intricacies of the social and legal constructions of fatherhood. This chapter is predominantly concerned with the various social and legal constructions of the non-residential father and associated representations thereof. I will consider how fathers with an interest in

---

1. If the non-residential father has his child to stay for more than 104 nights in a twelve-month period, then he becomes a person with care. The standard formula is adjusted downwards Reg. 1(2) CS(MASC) Regs. as amended by Reg. 40(2)(a) CS(MA)2 Regs.

showing themselves as the 'good fathers' of law have rigorously challenged the pernicious representations. My main focus here is upon how the non-residential father is constructed as 'absent' in social and legal discourses on child support. Moreover, I am also concerned to demonstrate how the representation of the non-residential father as 'absent' becomes problematized in law because of the influence of a variety of pedagogic disciplines (especially the 'psy' disciplines), which characterize the 'absent' father as just that – absent in every way. However, it is vital to note that not all instances of father absence are constructed in a negative manner. For example, psychoanalytical discourse regards paternal absence for the sake of paid work as an integral part of the fathering role. The next section of this chapter will examine how some instances of father absence are rendered legitimate by social and legal discourses. The following section will go on to consider how paternal 'absence' has come to be problematized in contemporary debates about fathering generally and child support in particular. In the recent debates about child support, the government in particular has lambasted the non-residential father as 'feckless' and 'irresponsible'. The latter part of the chapter will consider how the non-residential father is constructed in discourses about child support as 'absent', therefore 'bad'. It will then reveal the manner in which non-residential fathers have inverted the negative representations and used them to exonerate themselves of the charge of absence and also for the political end of bringing about reform to the Child Support Act.

Legitimate(d) father absence?

Academic, particularly psychoanalytical, theories have tended to sanction a degree of father absence for the sake of ensuring successful filial development. In some factions of men's studies that draw upon psychoanalytical perspectives, problems with father lack are identified as existing in the traditional nuclear family environment. Horrocks argues that due to changes in social and economic conditions (notably here the transformations brought about by the agricultural and industrial revolutions) there was a split of work and home whereby men became engaged in work in factories and offices. The father became a 'sepulchral' figure who returned only in time to see his children go to bed. While he claims that separation from the father is critical for the development of the *son's* male identity, if the association is too weak then 'boys are left floundering, unsure what it means to be a man, desperately short of male wisdom, male support and so on' (Horrocks 1994: 77–8). In his book, Horrocks uses sociological and literary analysis along with his experiences as a psycho-therapist in order to establish that masculinity is in crisis.

Another writer to point out the risk of the father's under-involvement in the son's life is psychologist Robert Bly. The phenomenon of father lack is again attributed to the increasing demands of paid work:

> By 1950, a massive change had taken place: the father works, but the son cannot see how he works, with whom he works, or what he produces. Does the son fantasise that his father is a lord, does he fill in positive details of the father's work place and the father's actions there, idealising his father as a hero, a fighter for good, a saint or grand person? The answer is sad: a hole appears in the son's psyche, a hole that fills with demons.   (Bly 1990: 3)

Bly also stresses the importance of the father/son relationship. His main emphasis is upon the idea that industrialization has caused there to be 'not enough father' (*ibid*.: 1) because of the increase in time spent away from the home. As a result, the son is forced to imagine the father for he cannot know him in his absence. According to Bly, the consequences of this for the son can be extremely depressing. The son may come to disparage all masculine achievement, rebel against his father, become weak and manipulated by women and other men and accept 'betrayal and humiliation under cover of teaching' (*ibid*.: 4). Both views are pessimistic about the future of fatherhood in the industrial world, particularly in relation to the father/son bond. The focus upon the centrality of the father/son relationship is typical of the fixation of the 'psy' disciplines with the importance of this filial relationship. It is also representative of the view that the boy must learn from his father the necessary skills to partake in the public world. Underpinning Horrocks's view is the assumption that a boy's future lies in his participation in the public world of work, which necessitates a 'break' from the home and the mother's influence.

It is clear that according to 'psy' discourses too weak an association between father and son leaves the son unsure of how to be a man. The role of the father then is to 'initiate the boy into manhood, into the world of men, where he can assume his identity as a man' (Horrocks 1994: 77). During industrialization in the early nineteenth century, the world of men became one that existed in a work environment outside the family home. The father's role became one of passing on to his sons the knowledge of how to survive in the outside world, for it was they and not his daughters who were destined to follow his footsteps (Rotundo 1987). Through these changing institutional work practices, a man's role came to be defined by his participation in the public world of work. At the same time, his role as father came to be defined as the family provider. Father was expected not only to make ample financial provision for all his family but also to furnish his sons with the requisite knowledge to pursue their own careers. A daughter, by contrast, becomes a woman 'by following in her mother's footsteps' (Rosaldo 1974: 28).

The importance of the relationship between children and the same-sex parent was stressed in the 1960s and 1970s. Rutter (1966), for example, argued that boys were likelier than girls to show psychiatric disorder if the father had died or was mentally ill. In a later book, he cites other work that claims to establish that delinquency rates are higher in boys if the father is absent from the home, but in girls the rate is higher if the mother is missing. He claims that such studies show the importance of the 'special role of the same-sexed parent' (Rutter 1972: 110–20). Psychological sex role theories have, however, been demonstrated as intellectually flawed as they fail to take full account of the significance and potential impact of *culturally* defined constructions of gender. In the early seventies, Ann Oakley (1972) revealed the oppressive nature of gender role stereotypes, stating them to be overwhelmingly coercive in their effects. Drawing upon these earlier feminist arguments, contemporary writers on masculinity have noted that men's gender stereotypes are also oppressive, culminating in men being conditioned into competitive, emotionally repressed and uncommunicative existences, often at the cost of their 'true' selves (Seidler 1994: 149). Additionally, they suggest that social and economic changes must have impacted upon the importance and significance of the father/son relationship. Rising male unemployment, increasing female employment outside the home and improvements in women's social status serve to undermine the centrality of the father/son relationship.

Notwithstanding the above reservations and weaknesses in sex role theory, the *idea* of its importance is still prevalent today. As Collier (1995a) has noted, it is through the divisions of public/private and work/home, and particularly in the way that masculinity is defined by reference to a man's economic capacity, that the physical absence of fathers from the home is justified in family law. He eloquently demonstrates, using a number of custody cases, how the tenacity of the idea of the centrality of the father's breadwinner function remains entrenched in legal decisions. What is more, the Child Support Act reinforces the importance of the father's duty to maintain his family by using the notion of parental responsibility to fix the financial responsibility for children firmly with their biological fathers. To this extent, the Child Support Act concerns itself with enforcing the notion that the non-residential father's appropriate role is to provide financially for his children. Thus, the fathering role is reduced to a mere economic nexus (*ibid.*).

According to this reasoning, physical father absence is rendered more acceptable by the government if in his absence the father makes the requisite remuneration for his children's upkeep. However, recent political and social trends and developments in the various academic disciplines have rendered the reduction of fathering to a mere economic nexus – the lesser of two evils. The non-residential father who makes the requisite financial contribution to his children's upkeep is regarded as superior and preferable to the non-residential father who does not. He has at least some presence, due to the meeting of his financial obligation to the children. It also becomes possible for him to argue that he is not the 'feckless' father of popular discourse. However, recent discourses have generated the idea that the father should have more presence than arises from his purely financial contribution. Active, participating fatherhood has become the norm to which fathers should aspire.

Problematizing father absence in lone parent households

Legal and social discourses represent the non-presence of the paterfamilias as problematic in a number of ways. In law, the very employment of the term 'absent' used in statutes and discussion documents carries with it negative connotations. Etymologically, the word derives from the Latin word 'abesse', which means 'to be away'. It is a term that can also arguably be said to imply a derogation of duty, non-existence, nothingness. The first volume of the White Paper preceding the Child Support Act 1991, *Children Come First*, highlights the importance of not allowing the non-residential parent to escape his obligations of care for his children:

> Every child has a right to care from his or her parents. Parents
> generally have a legal and moral obligation to care for their children
> until the children are old enough to look after themselves.
>
> The parents of a child may separate. In some instances the
> parents may not have lived together as a family at all. Although
> events may change the relationships between the parents – for
> example when they divorce – those events cannot in any way change
> their responsibilities towards their children.   (HMSO 1990: Foreword)

It is instructive that despite the government's use of the term 'absent' in the ensuing statute, the White Paper embraces the principle that non-residential fathers should maintain their relationships with their children in much the same vein as before the family breakdown. In other words, the government uses the concept of continuing parental responsibility to emphasize the importance of father presence in instances where they no longer physically reside with their children. Nearly two years after the Act's implementation, the government restated its commitment to the principle that parents should retain the responsibility for children and should not attempt to offload the responsibility onto the state (*ibid.*: 11). The then Conservative government responded to the oft-made complaint that fathers were unable to maintain close contact with their children because of increased child support payments.[2] Under new rules, those non-residential parents who qualified for a departure from the formula were allowed to have the costs of travel to see their children taken into consideration in the assessment of maintenance when those costs were exceptionally high (*ibid.*: para. 2.6). This change can be interpreted in a number of ways. It might be viewed as consolidating the government's commitment to ensuring that paternal contact with children is maintained. Alternatively, the change might be considered as part of a package of changes that attempted to appease the mass of middle-class fathers who voiced their grievances about the Act in a vociferous manner. Less cynically, perhaps, it could have been a very real attempt to respond to the problems caused by the inflexibility of the formula. Whatever the motivation for the re-introduction of discretion into the formula, the change has had the effect of highlighting the desirability of maintaining links between a father and his child(ren).

Father 'absence' is the opposite of all that is now held sacrosanct in many contemporary discourses on the modern family. These discourses are generated by a number of disparate sources, from the relatively new faction of 'men's studies' to psychology, the media, sociology and politics (Collier 1995b). As Collier has observed, however, the grouping together of a body of work on masculinity under a single umbrella of men's studies is erroneous due to the heterogeneous nature of the writings on the subject (1995a). The phrase is used here only as a means of capturing the diversity of disciplinary interest.

---

2. The Social Security Committee's fifth report revealed that it had received over 400 letters of complaint from non-residential fathers about the inflexibility of the formula used to calculate the maintenance assessment. One of the main complaints was that it did not take account of the expenses incurred by the father in maintaining contact with his children. Reported in *The Guardian*, 3 November 1993.

For example, the political right wing proclaimed its desire for a return to that mythical 'golden age', where the traditional two-parent family resided together and practised mutual support. Feminists have argued for men's greater participation in child rearing in the name of eliminating the sexual division of labour in the home. Men's groups have sought to establish their 'rights' to greater involvement in childcare both before and after divorce. Psychologists and sociologists alike have warned of the dangers of paternal deprivation. In relation to criminological discourse, it is the absence of the father that 'denies these essentially "barbarian" young boys a suitable masculine role model' (Collier 1998: 130). According to Collier, in the articulation of the underclass theory in Britain from the mid-1990s to the present day, there is an

> Increasing prominence of the explicit association which is being made between family breakdown, crime and the more general notion of a crisis of masculinity in which, crucially, the concept of fatherhood has moved centre-stage. (1998: 131)

While the motivations for debates around the desired presence or absence of fathers in families may be various, they all share a commonality of theme. The common motif constructed by these discourses is the problematic nature of the *lack* or absence of the father figure. However, it is worth restating that a *degree* of father absence is frequently justified in the name of a man providing financially for his family and also in supplying his sons with the appropriate role model. Notwithstanding the legitimation of this degree of father absence, the absence should not be excessive. Notwithstanding legitimate father absence, there are still problems associated with the lack of a father's influence within the traditional family environment. The problem is regarded as potentially more threatening and pernicious for the family where the father is constructed as absent in a complete sense, in physical, emotional, moral and financial terms, notably here, in those families where the parents are separated or divorced.

Constructing the 'feckless father'

In enacting its new legislation on child support, the government claimed to be responding to a situation that it maintained had become unacceptable. Non-residential fathers were regarded as failing in their duties to maintain their offspring financially. The Child Support Act was established to reinstate parental financial responsibility wherever it was perceived to be lacking. During the Act's first year of operation, the media followed its fortunes with dogged interest. Alistair Burt (then junior social security minister responsible for the CSA) was prompted to argue that the media were responsible for 'fuelling a campaign of hate and intimidation against its staff' (*The Guardian*, 18 May 1993). Newspaper coverage included articles written from a variety of perspectives. A number of articles did present a sympathetic outlook towards non-residential fathers in relation to how they were being treated by the Child Support Agency. Headlines and sub-headlines read: 'Fathers who are reduced to paupers' (*The Independent on Sunday*, 19 September 1993); 'CSA letter "caused suicide"' (*The Guardian*, 25 November 1994); 'Child Support Agency "delaying" fathers' appeals' (*The Guardian*, 15 December 1994); 'Tripled maintenance payments "led to divorcee's death"' (*The Guardian*, 7 December 1993).

The media were extravagant in highlighting the inefficacy of the CSA with regard to its treatment of non-residential fathers. And Burt was explicit in his recognition of the potency of the media. He was claiming that the press was contributing positively to the way the Child Support Act was perceived both by the general public and by particular individuals. In concurrence with Burt, I would argue that press coverage has played a major part in successfully constructing the non-residential father as the victim of an unfair and badly administered law. But he neglects to point to other articles that provide a portrayal of non-residential fathers far removed from the sympathetic cameos above. A number of articles appeared that highlighted the 'social crisis' taking place because of the decline in the traditional family and the accompanying rise in the lone parent family. In many if not the majority of instances of this kind of coverage, the central focus of the media coverage was the lone mother, but a significant number of articles pinpointed the blame for the decline in the traditional family on 'feckless fathers' (*The Independent on Sunday*, 14 November 1993).

Many articles focused upon the problems caused by 'feckless' working-class fathers who abandon the women they have 'impregnated' and then shirk all their corresponding familial responsibilities to the woman and child. Blake Morrison wrote that men have become 'unburdened' by the contraceptive pill. If women assume control over contraception by way of taking the pill, if they then become pregnant what responsibility has the father to the mother and the child? While he does not use the inflammatory image of the 'feckless' father, he does hold that as long as men are able to shirk their responsibilities they will continue to do so. In Morrison's view, the Child Support Act is needed to prevent men 'denying . . . children basic financial support' (*The Independent on Sunday*, 9 January 1994).

Some of these articles drew their influence from academic writers of both left- and right-wing thought. From the left of the political spectrum came the work of Halsey, Dennis and Erdos. And from the right, Charles Murray, an American writer who has been credited with providing the intellectual basis for the Conservative government's 'back to basics' campaign. Morrison's account of irresponsible fathers echoes the work of Dennis and Erdos, who argue that once women were able to manage without men then men naturally absconded from fatherhood. Once the 'onerous tasks' of parenthood 'became avoidable . . . it was quite natural that fatherhood was increasingly avoided'. According to this thesis, it is feminism and other intellectual libertarians that are to blame for male irresponsibility. There is no point in attempting to look towards poverty as an explanation of the general social malaise (Dennis and Erdos 1992). Other articles about the 'feckless father' were based upon interviews with individual lone mothers and their own accounts of the men who were the biological fathers of their children (see *The Times*, 7 July 1993; *Daily Telegraph*, 7 July 1993; and *Daily Telegraph*, 5 July 1993).

One such story appeared in *The Times*. A lone mother told the story of how her partner had left her after she had given birth to their daughter: 'I could tell that my boy friend wasn't willing to face up to the responsibility of fatherhood. Then one day he found an escape route – he just walked out and left us.' The mother's depressed reaction to her partner's departure finally resulted in her attempting to commit suicide. Her initial response was a deep feeling of loss on behalf of her daughter and herself (*The Times*, 7 July 1993). A theme running through many of these discourses is the idea that children from lone parent families are not only 'lacking' a father but also that they, and society generally, are 'suffering' from that deficit. Charles Murray, a right-wing American sociologist (who it has been reported influenced the government's campaign against lone parenthood) has warned of the dangers of the rising numbers of lone parent households. According to Murray, illegitimacy is problematic because children who have never had fathers lack discipline and appropriate role models.

Murray's ideas are by no means innovative. As was highlighted above, the 'psy' theories of the 1960s and 1970s discussed fathering in terms of role playing and serving as role models for children. It remains the case that latter-day theories also stress the importance of appropriate role models for children. Then as now, such ideas promote the belief that there is something distinctive or special about the fathering role. Women who decide (or are left) to bring up children alone are subjected to the notion that they are inadequately equipped to perform all the requisite roles. In *The Independent on Sunday*, Murray is quoted as saying:

> In a neighbourhood where few adult males are playing the traditional role of father, the most impressive man around is likely to teach all of the opposite lessons: sleep with as many women as you can, rip off the money you need and to hell with the rules, waste anyone who gets in your face.   (9 January 1994)

Clearly, one of Murray's main concerns about lone parent families is the lack or absence of the appropriate 'father figure'. According to Murray, father absence on a large scale leads to a 'serious social problem'. The importance of the father for the teaching of psychological, social, moral and economic lessons is emphasized: 'a liberal society depends on virtue and self-restraint in the people, and the family, *traditionally* construed, is the place where the stuff of a free society is moulded' (*ibid.*, my italics).

The father is a *sine qua non* not only for the well-being of the family but also for society generally. Implicit in Murray's rhetoric are a number of other themes worth highlighting. In his opinion, anything that falls outside the traditional nuclear family is incapable of providing the appropriate role models for children and is thus rendered a deviant family form. His work also has a racial dimension as he brings into question the efficacy of the non-traditional family form as a means of raising children. For example, he casts doubt upon the extended family common among African-Americans, insisting that marriage is the only institution that brings family cohesion. Additionally, Murray's work can clearly be seen to be anti-feminist if we go on to consider, as Beatrix Campbell does, the absence from his thesis of any recognition of the practical and emotional work of women as carers. She maintains that Murray's thesis is remarkable for the invisibility of women, mothers, grandmothers, aunts, 'as the real, live, operational carers' (Campbell 1993: 309).

His much-expounded view is that single parenthood is neither an economically viable nor a socially acceptable option. In short, lone mothers are regarded as incapable of adequately performing all the requisite functions to bring up a child successfully. According to Murray, welfare support should be withdrawn from the lone mother so she would be forced to rely on other, more economically and socially viable, options such as adoption, her family or presumably the fathers from whom the women may be seeking to escape. Ideally, in Murray's view, the withdrawal of benefits from lone mothers would induce women into more socially acceptable alliances and dissuade women from embarking upon the increasingly willing course of having babies without marrying. He argues:

> The closest thing to a cultural constant throughout human history, until a few decades ago, has been that a single woman with a small child is not a viable economic unit; and that not being a viable economic unit, neither is the single woman with a child a legitimate social unit.   (*The Independent on Sunday*, 9 January 1994)

In his appraisal of the problematic nature of the lone parent family form, the key motifs are the increasing willingness of women to have children alone and the failure of men to fulfil their paternal and matrimonial duties. In other words, it would seem that Murray is constructing the problem as revolving around two poles. The first is concerned with what he perceives to be women's increasing 'willingness' to embark on having children outside marriage. Here, women who go on to have children outside marriage are constructed as being over-active or unruly in their sexual behaviour.[3] This unruly behaviour is regarded as best contained by the marriage institution. Correspondingly, men's sexual behaviour can also be said to be in need of containment in Murray's thesis, but it is not the restriction of men's sexual behaviour that is his primary concern. Rather, this leads on to the second set of ideas implicit in his work.

Although men's over-activity in sexual matters is problematized in Murray's thesis, men are additionally constructed as reneging on their paternal duties. They are failing to provide their children with suitable role models or adequate financial support, and are lacking in some or all ways. In other words, Murray is constructing the non-residential father as 'inactive'. And for Murray and other social commentators, it is this inactivity or passivity in relation to fatherhood that is problematic. Men are represented as feckless and lacking in moral responsibility to their children and as deliberately trying to evade their financial responsibilities. They are neither appropriate role models for their children nor their financial providers. Rather, they are constituted as failing in their duties to produce and sustain 'normal' children.[4] Men who are regarded as reneging on their paternal financial responsibilities are represented as transgressing the culturally generated norms of the polarities of woman/man, mother/father and passive/active.

---

3. It is not the first time that women have been constructed as 'the unruly feminine'. See Smart 1992.
4. This issue is raised in Smart 1991.

The Child Support Act attempts to reinforce paternal participation and make up some of the ground lost through what is regarded as father passivity by guaranteeing the financial bond between fathers and their children. Non-residential fathers, in seeking the abolition of the Act, have argued that it goes little way towards attempting to enforce the concept of ongoing parental responsibility in the sense of offering practical support for the continuance of the familial relationship based upon emotional and moral support. In effect, non-residential fathers are able to make the claim that the Act is more concerned with recouping money for the Treasury's coffers than with securing ongoing familial relationships. For example, non-residential father Nigel Sheppard was reported as saying: 'Its not for the benefit of children, but to bring in money for the Treasury' (*The Guardian*, 3 November 1994). This comment was typical of the welter of comments made by non-residential fathers in the first years of the Act's operation. At the same time, non-residential fathers also sought to demonstrate that their own priorities lay with sustaining mutually rewarding and beneficial relationships with their children. Their claims derive support and potency from discourses that advocate the merits of active fathering. It is to this matter that I now turn.

The construction of a 'new' fatherhood

In the preceding sections of this chapter, I have demonstrated how legal and social discourses about child support have constructed father absence around the motifs of lack, inactivity or passivity in relation to paternal responsibility in the post-separation context. I have also argued that the 'psy' discourses have been critical of too little father presence in the context of the traditional two-parent family. The problematization of the absent father has given rise to a set of discourses that advocate father participation as the norm to which fathers should aspire. In order to be seen to be fulfilling his paternal obligation, the 'good' father has to demonstrate his commitment to active fathering.

In the 1950s and 1960s, the discourses generated by the 'psy' disciplines emphasized the importance of the mother for the continued well-being of the child. Perhaps the most famous proponent of this view was John Bowlby. He argued that 'mother love in infancy and childhood is as important for mental health as are vitamins and proteins for physical health' (Bowlby 1951: 125).

According to Bowlby's formulation, the attachment between a mother and her child is essential for the child's mental well-being. He maintained that the bond between a mother and her child is special and different in kind from the ones forged with others (*ibid.*). Bowlby's work came to be extremely influential, effecting changes in the hospitalization of children; influencing psychological theorizing; drawing attention to the need to explain the characteristics of the mother/child bond; and giving rise to strongly held views, often from polarized positions (*ibid.*: editorial foreword).

By the 1970s, the adequacy of 'attachment' and 'maternal deprivation' theories were under challenge from new research, which demonstrated that infants could form attachments with a variety of people and not just the mother (Lewis 1982). Maternal deprivation theory came to be supplemented by the theory of 'paternal deprivation'. For example, Biller (1971) argued that children who forged relationships with adults of only one sex are at a disadvantage later with respect to heterosexual relationships and to the development of sex-appropriate attitudes and behaviour. According to Rutter, it became widely held that for

> optimal development [of the child] bonds needed to be formed with people of *both* sexes, and from what has been said about attachment behaviour it is very likely that early attachments will influence the kind of close relationships which are possible later.
>
> (1972: 106; italics are the author's)

The importance of the father/child relationship for the child's successful development was now being stressed in the discourses of the 'psy' disciplines. Later research was also revealing a stated desire by middle-class fathers to participate actively in childcare. Margaret O'Brien revealed that middle-class men who articulated a belief in shared parenting expressed 'high or fairly high' levels of work–home conflict, even though they did very little to put their belief in shared childcare responsibility to practical effect (O'Brien 1982). Here, though, I am not interested in the merits of one theory over another or the extent to which fathers actually do actively participate in child rearing, for this has been done elsewher (Lewis and O'Brien 1987). Rather, my interest lies in the way that these new theories/discourses influence the debates surrounding the (un)desirability of the non-residential father and, further, how the idea of the new participant father (as opposed to the simply present father) has been used by non-residential fathers in the campaign against the Child Support Act.

Father participation has been advocated from many quarters. As has been demonstrated above, the 'psy' disciplines and sociology have stressed the importance of the father as role model for developing children, particularly sons. Feminists too have supported the idea of greater father participation in the hope of breaking with a tradition of the gendered division of labour in the home. For example, in 1972 Rachel Wortis argued that if women's under-valuation in society is to end then a more equitable distribution of the labour in the home and in child rearing must be effected (Wortis 1972: 127–30). By the end of the 1970s, Nancy Chodorow was also advocating dual parenting. Drawing upon psychoanalytical object relations psychology, she highlighted the problematic nature of exclusive mothering by women in the creation and perpetuation of male dominance and the development of polarized masculine and feminine identities. According to Chodorow, if dual parenting were to become the prevalent practice, then a boy raised partly by the father would not develop fears of maternal power or 'expectations of women's unique self-sacrificing qualities'. Traditional masculine and feminine roles would be supplanted by roles that could be performed adequately by males or females, with girls and boys having an expectation that both men and women would be caring. At the same time, women would also be considered, along with men, to be autonomous. The result, according to Chodorow, might be that boys would no longer have to reject the feeling of nurturance, for it would no longer be viewed as a feminine characteristic (Chodorow 1978: 218).

Active fathering is also put forward by the various factions of men's studies as the best means of ensuring the well-being of the father of the family. In addition to the older ideas of the father as the necessary role model for his children (and in particular his sons), the 'new father' was being represented by some writers interested in men's studies as someone who sought to make an emotional investment in his children. This investment was constructed as beneficial to both the child and the father. According to Pogrebin (1981), the child would benefit through the father's avoidance of the sex-role stereotypes regarded as so crucial to earlier ideas propounded by the 'psy' disciplines. By practising participant fatherhood, men could avoid the traditional stereotypes in dealing with their own children. Girls would benefit from encouragement to be competitive in all spheres, and boys could be encouraged to develop a stronger emotional bond with their own subsequent children through the patterns set by the 'modern' father (Rotundo 1987).

Men would benefit from developing intense emotional relationships and from sharing 'a more expressive and intimate relationship than men of previous generations'. Some writers in men's studies have recognized that the desirability of changing conceptions of appropriate fathering have been brought about by feminism. As such, they can be perceived as responding in a sympathetic manner to the demands set by a feminist agenda. One such writer, Seidler, notes that it has 'taken feminism and psychotherapy' (and I would add sociology and psychology) to remind men of the 'value' of familial relationships and also of the time and energy that is necessary to sustain them. He encourages men to recognize that meaningful relationships with children have 'to be every day, not just at weekends (Seidler 1994: 149–50). In this and other writings, he is advocating more active participation by fathers in order that the man might discover his true self (Seidler 1988).

Valuable relationships between men and their children are regarded as beneficial both to children and to their fathers and also to the relationships between women and men. Seidler seeks to address the impoverishment of emotion that is so often associated with masculinity. In an earlier work, he argues that while men might hear women's cries of anger and frustration, and while they may well understand them intellectually, men continuously find it difficult to accept that the situation can really be that bad (Seidler 1985). His more recent writings incorporate an optimistic note about the potential for change. The earlier work above, by contrast, is pessimistic in tone and seems to accept almost fatalistically men's inability to change.

Changes in fatherhood practice are very firmly on the agenda of Jeff Hearn. He maintains that men should attempt to transform the relationship between men and their children by getting rid of the notion (and indeed the practices) of the authoritarian father. Instead, Hearn advocates the breaking down of the distinction of children that men live with and children that live outside the family unit, so that men work not just upon developing relationships with their 'own' children but with all children. The aim is to develop friendly relationships with all children and not just relationships based upon the narrowly defined paternal affiliation. He thus problematizes fatherhood from his own personal experience, which stems from

> a material involvement, doing work for children and a slow realisation
> that the potential of relationships with children is enhanced by
> getting away from fatherhood. Instead of relying on the authority of
> the father, we can better work towards forms of responsible friendship
> with children.   (Hearn 1987: 158)

Hearn's critique is based upon the notion that the structured paternal relationship is inherently oppressive. He advocates the assumption of relationships with a variety of children, not just one's own through the institution of fatherhood. Hearn's critique of fatherhood is radical in that he encourages men to renounce their privileged position of power under patriarchy and that which results from their social status as fathers. Instead, he encourages men to form meaningful relationships with children both inside and outside the family environment. He is keen for men to avoid the paternal relationship based upon the authority of the father. It can be argued that what Hearn is seeking to do is to formulate a new way in which men can interact with children. At the same time, he advocates an extension of men's relationships with children to include children outside the home. As a result, Hearn can be interpreted as seeking to reconstruct the role of the father to include greater participation in children's lives rather than eradicating the notion of fatherhood. Moreover, he also seeks to extend the father's dominion by encouraging active participation in other children's lives. In summary, though Hearn might reject the notion of father as traditionally constructed, he suggests an alternative construction of fatherhood rather than rejecting the concept altogether.

Contemporary discourses on fathering, though emanating from multifarious theoretical standpoints and disciplines, all laud the idea of the participant father. While the ideology of the male breadwinner is still prevalent in discourses about the family, wherein father absence is justified for the sake of providing for one's children, father's physical presence in the home is now simply not enough. Fathers must also *actively* contribute to their children's upbringing in an emotional and physical way. Where that emotional and physical relationship can be demonstrated as being denied or obliterated, fathers are given the opportunity to raise the debate about fatherhood on the terms of lack of contact with children as being a denial of a 'right' to a beneficial and productive relationship with their children. Again, the purpose here is not to debate the extent to which active participation and a more equal sharing of child-rearing duties has been effected in practice. Rather, it is my interest here to examine the manner in which constructing fatherhood as a mutually beneficial relationship between fathers and their children has served to propagate the view that both children and non-residential fathers 'suffer' from the enforced denial of this relationship. And, moreover, I aim to demonstrate how fathers are able to show themselves as victims of the Child Support Act by portraying the Act as exacerbating their already vulnerable father/child relationship.

Constructing the climate for change

In this final section, I hope to demonstrate the terms upon which non-residential fathers have brought about reforms of the Child Support

Act, and at a maximum to have it abolished. It will also be asserted that the terms upon which non-residential fathers have based their struggle against the Act derive their potency from the fathers' ability to show themselves as the victims of negative and 'false' discourses. They also portray themselves as the victims of an unfair and overly intrusive piece of legislation, the Child Support Act, which has the potential to undermine rather than reinforce the paternal relationship. The media have also been instrumental in constructing non-residential fathers as victims. In *The Independent on Sunday*, non-residential father Chris Chambers told how increased maintenance demands by the Child Support Agency had meant that he could no longer afford to see his estranged children regularly due to the high cost of travel and the burden of the increased child support. He is quoted as saying:

> If I can't afford to see her except on special occasions, I'll lose
> involvement in her life which matters to both of us. Without regular,
> normal contact I am sure our relationship will suffer. If Rebecca
> becomes an occasional visitor, apart from losing the intimacy she
> has with me, she will also lose it with her new brother and sister
> who adore her.   (*The Independent on Sunday*, 19 September 1993)

Of course, Mr Chambers's stated commitment to his daughter Rebecca can be applauded, and it is not my intention to denounce or undermine it. There can be no argument against the promotion of a loving, caring, functional relationship between a parent and his or her child in the absence of conflict between the parties in question. Rather, my point here is that the *idea* (if not necessarily the practice) of the mutually beneficial father/child emotional relationship is so prevalent and so widely accepted, and that infringement of it is viewed as a breach of a right of both the father and the child. The above cameo also tells the story of a breach being caused between the child of the first family and the children of the second family. The increased burden of child support resulting from the intervention of the Child Support Agency is held responsible for undermining family life as reconstituted through divorce and re-partnership.

Newspapers also gave voice to members of various fathers' support groups. One of the groups that was most prominently represented in the press was Families Need Fathers (FNF), which seeks to protect the rights of fathers in the post-separation or divorce context. In *The Guardian* in 1993, Trevor Berry of FNF was cited as saying that most fathers who did not pay maintenance simply could not afford it. At the same time, he argued that fathers would have a tougher time getting access to children. He was quoted thus:

> There is no doubt that in the real world the issues of access and money are closely related. The CSA will sever the link and fathers will be powerless.   (*The Guardian*, 19 January 1993)

The article does not fully develop what is meant about the link that allegedly exists between 'access' (now contact) and money. However, it seems reasonable to assume that he refers to the manner in which non-residential fathers are unable to sustain contact due to their increased expenditure on child support. What is also interesting about Berry's statement is that he refers to the feelings of powerlessness experienced as a result of the intervention of the Child Support Agency. According to Berry, the Child Support Act not only caused problems of contact for him and his children, it also made a further inroad into the balance of power between mothers and fathers, which FNF argues has swung too far towards protecting the rights of mothers. Bruce Lidington, the chairman of FNF, writes:

> Non custodial fathers are one of the most vulnerable sections of society, most are financially and emotionally exhausted by the divorce process and, with the possible exception of Families Need Fathers, have no organised way of challenging any untruths published by powerful interests.   (Lidington 1992: 22)

Lidington argues that non-residential fathers are already financially and emotionally vulnerable due to divorce. Additionally, he claims that the voices of non-residential fathers have become marginalized by the discourses of those with 'powerful interests'. Lidington refers here to the government's interest in raising money to meet the cost of child support. He argues that non-residential fathers are thus rendered insecure due to divorce and also because of the interest of the state in recouping funds for the Treasury's coffers. According to Lidington and his supporters, non-residential fathers are victims not only of the personal consequences of divorce but also of an overbearing state, which seeks to make them 'scape-goats' for the rising cost of child support. Moreover, Lidington is offended by the use of the term 'absent father'. He advises other group members thus:

> Every reader of this article . . . has been legally defined under the Child Support Act as an 'absent parent'!! I don't know about other readers but, even though I nowadays have an amicable and cooperative post-divorce situation, I find it offensive to be described as 'an absent father'. I am, as I always have been, here for my daughter. My daughter is absent from me. The use of this abusive term is equivalent to using the term 'cripple' in legislation for the disabled.
>   (*ibid.*: 22)

Non-residential father Tony Walentowicz echoed this view in another article that appeared in *The Guardian* in 1993:

> What I really object to is that they [the Child Support Agency] wrote to me as an absent father. That is really unfair. I've never ducked any of my responsibilities. I've always paid up. It's insulting to say that about me. There are thousands of others in my position . . . We fully recognise our responsibilities. But it seems we are the ones who will be hit hardest, while those who have done a runner will be quietly ignored.   (13 September 1993)

By highlighting the use of the term 'absent father' in the governing child support legislation, the above writers are able to use the offensive definition to position themselves in the debate as being the direct opposite of 'absent'. In other words, non-residential fathers use the term as one pole of two extremes. At one end, the term 'absent' contains extremely negative connotations. The non-residential father sites himself at the other end of the pole as a 'present' father and associates himself with all the positive aspects of father 'presence'. Despite the father's sometimes physical absence from the child, he is and will always be there for his child(ren). According to these fathers' discourses, the child support legislation constructs them in a negative manner. At the same time, they are also being treated unfairly by the state as the Child Support Agency targets middle-class fathers who already pay maintenance and participate in their children's lives rather than those fathers who have completely disappeared from their children's lives. Despite the inevitability of occasional physical absence from the child, the non-residential father presents himself as the lauded participating father of the modern day.[5]

Fathers' support groups seek to re-establish the notion of fathers' rights. These groups are endeavouring to swing the pendulum of change (which they maintain has gone too far towards favouring mothers) back towards recognizing the competing rights of the non-residential father. Their arguments are based upon the idea that family law has gone too far in protecting women's interests and that the law shows preference for mothers in issues about financial provision and custody decisions (Brophy 1985).

---

5. Throughout 1993 and 1994, many sympathetic accounts of the plight of middle-class fathers appeared in the national press. See, for example, *The Guardian*, 3 November 1994; *The Guardian*, 6 April 1994; *The Guardian*, 20 June 1994; *The Guardian*, 18 May 1994; *The Times*, 19 August 1993; *The Guardian*, 25 November 1994; *The Guardian*, 11 January 1994.

Research is often proffered by men's groups seeking to re-establish the notion of fathers' rights which claims that paternal deprivation is likely to lead to social problems such as juvenile crime, drug abuse, suicide and poor educational attainment.[6] Clearly, such claims serve to justify the reassertion of fathers' rights on the basis that children benefit from continuing relationships with the non-residential father. Fathers' groups also stress that it is not just the children who suffer as a result of a prolonged lack of contact. FNF suggests that the caring parent will sometimes work actively towards the total exclusion of the non-residential father. According to the group, the phenomenon is so virulent as to warrant classification as a syndrome, 'parental alienation syndrome' (PAS). FNF defines PAS thus:

> At one level it is simply a child picking up the mother's attitudes towards the father. Over a period of time the child learns not to mention the father, or share the joys and experiences had with him. At another level it is the obvious denigration of the father at every opportunity. At the extreme, the father may be falsely accused of physical or sexual abuse. It is an insidious form of emotional child abuse that is difficult to avoid between hostile parents.
>
> (FNF 1993)

According to FNF, PAS can take any of these forms. At the most serious level, the father might be 'falsely' accused of physical or sexual abuse. The other extreme is characterized by the child internalizing the mother's attitude towards the father. Central to both is the idea that it is the mother who is responsible for the process of parental (perhaps more appropriately paternal) alienation. The mother is 'blamed' for the lack of contact between the father and his child and the father's eventual estrangement. At the same time, the aspect of the abuse to the child is also emphasized. Again, putting forward PAS as a form of child abuse suggests that women are responsible for the perpetration of the harm occasioned by children as a result of the denigration of the father. Such allegations are inimical to the idea that mothers are capable of acting in the best interests of their children. Moreover, the establishment of parental estrangement as a problem is based upon the idea that paternal contact is always in the child's best interests when this may well not always be the case.

---

6. See, for example, paper on the 'Effects of divorce/separation' presented by M. Bell (Co-director of Both Parents Forever) at Exeter University, September 1992.

The suggestion that children and fathers suffer as a result of prolonged separation places fathers' rights closer to the interests of the children. As such, it acts as a 'direct counter claim to the strength of the assumption that child welfare is most secure in the hands of mothers' (Smart and Sevenhuijsen 1989: 9). Moreover, the non-residential father in opposition to the Child Support Act is provided with another source of useful ammunition with which to combat the Act. The government, the media and the general public can be lobbied for support on the grounds that the Child Support Act serves to deprive both the father and his children of the right to contact and its concomitant benefits for both the father/child relationship and for society as a whole. The non-residential father who can present himself as lacking in this contact because of the state's legislative intervention also presents himself as a victim of an unfair system. According to Chris Chambers and other non-residential fathers, they are the victims of an over-powerful state that is making excessive and unfair demands on their financial resources. Non-residential fathers campaigning against the Child Support Act are seeking to reclaim some of the bargaining power they felt they had in financial settlements on divorce before the Act's implementation. It has been noted by Brophy (1985) that while the law has never officially sanctioned 'trade-offs' between money and children, the negotiating process did provide the opportunity for parties to link money and custody.

Moreover, fathers have used the idea of the mutually beneficial father/child relationship to mobilize societal support against the government and ultimately the Child Support Act. The non-residential father's pleas for support of the continuance of the purported existing emotional relationship serves to highlight the truth that non-residential fathers are not feckless or lacking in their role model function. Rather, they remain 'family' men committed to the perpetuation of their familial relationships. Fathers' support groups, which have been growing in number and type since the implementation of the Act,[7] respond to government, academic and media accusations of absence and fecklessness by stating their innocence with regard to the charges made against them. Moreover, FNF and DAD argue that the Child Support Act is yet another example of the trend towards weakening or eroding the status of the non-residential

7. Network Against the Child Support Act; Payday Men's Network (part of the Campaign Against the Child Support Act); Cover Against Parental Exploitation; National Campaign for Fair Maintenance; all joining men's groups that existed before the implementation of the Act – DAD and FNF.

father on divorce or separation. In other words, men are portrayed as becoming increasingly disempowered by recent legislative trends, and pressure groups such as the above are mourning the loss of male legal authority in the realm of the familial. The alleged disempowerment of men is aligned with the 'crisis of masculinity' thesis as described by Collier (1998: 131, cited above).

It is true to say that there has indeed been a legal erosion of the eighteenth-century notion of 'father right' whereby the father had exclusive legal rights over his wife and family, which began with the Guardianship of Minors Act 1925. However, the extent to which courts do show maternal preference as far as custody issues are concerned is highly debatable, especially in those cases where some shortfall on the part of the mother can be demonstrated (Brophy 1985). To this extent, the existence of a judicial maternal preference in custody cases as propounded by FNF may be more symbolic than real. The antipathy felt by men's pressure groups towards the Child Support Act can thus be seen as part of a broad canvas of hostility to the slight but significant shift in the balance of power between women and men.

In contemporary Western society, women have succeeded in attaining greater control over their own sexuality and fertility than in previous times.[8] Technological advances have given rise to the opportunity for women to have children without the trappings of conventional male/female relationships, and there seems to be some small progress in getting courts to legitimize these alternative family forms by giving lesbian parents full parental responsibility (case reported in *The Guardian*, 2 July 1994). Also, courts in this country have thus far upheld the idea that abortion is an issue between a woman and her doctors. They have also resisted attempts by fathers to attain legal standing in decisions relating to abortion (Paton *v.* BPAS [1979] QB 276; C *v.* S [1987] 1 All ER 1230). Since the divorce law reform of 1969, which culminated in the Matrimonial Causes Act 1973, women have consistently made more use of the relaxed law than have men. In 1971, women filed 67,000 petitions for divorce, compared with 44,000 by men. By 1989, the figure for women had more than doubled to 135,000, while the figure for men had risen by only 6,000 to 50,000 (Social Trends 1991: 21.5). The figures indicate, despite the belief common at the time that the majority of petitioners would be men, that women were increasingly keen to escape their matrimonial burden in spite of the

---

8. Although lesbian women frequently resort to informal arrangements, which are not recognized as being exempt from the rules of the Child Support Act, because they fear refusal by the state-registered clinics.

resulting financial and social penalties. Furthermore, research has also demonstrated that in recent years women are more inclined to embark upon having children outside marriage than was the case in previous years. In 1979, the total of live births outside marriage was 69,000. By 1992, the figure had risen to 215,200. Notwithstanding this increase, the number of births registered by both parents has risen from 50 per cent in 1979 to 76.1 per cent in 1992, with 50 per cent registered by both parents living at the same address (NCOPF 1994). It is clear that half of the births occurring outside marriage can be accounted for by couples who elect to cohabit rather than marry, but it remains the case that the other half must consist of individuals who have chosen or been forced into alternative family arrangements. Marriage is no longer the main option for women and men who choose to have children. The contemporary family is marked by diversity and includes lesbian and homosexual couples and lone parent households (in the main, dominated by female heads). Women are electing to have and raise children alone or with other women. As a concomitant, men's stranglehold over women's potential for child bearing and rearing is being weakened. Some men, worried at the perceived prospect of losing authority in the realm of the familial, are reasserting the notion of father right. They are also challenging perceived trends that indicate a shift in power away from them and towards women (at least in the sphere of control over childbirth and child rearing). As Collier has noted, men are constructed as the 'victims' of a feminism that has gone 'too far' in unbalancing hitherto 'equal rights' (1995b: 6). He also rightly observes that by thus constructing men as 'victims' of a progressive feminism, the cultural climate in which gendered formations of masculinity and the changing representations of fatherhood are reproduced are neglected (*ibid.*).

Summary '

This chapter has examined some of the discourses that have constructed the non-residential father as 'absent' and also therefore as a problem. It has also considered the significance of these discourses for what appears to have been a consolidated struggle by non-residential fathers to overturn the Child Support Act. The word 'struggle' depicts how those non-residential fathers involved in campaigning against the Act have managed (with effective help from the media) to construct themselves as endeavouring in the face of adversity to overcome the mighty force of an intrusive, over-zealous state that is out to ruin their lives. In effect, non-residential fathers have successfully portrayed themselves as the *victims* of an unjust and immoderate law. Moreover, the discourses that have been responsible for constituting the non-residential father as a problem have been taken up by separated and divorced fathers and used to confirm their victim status.

Paradoxically, this ability to show themselves as victims of both an unjust law and of negative discourses that construct non-residential fathers as feckless has provided these fathers, as a group, with a position of strength. The deluge of social and legal representations of the non-residential father as feckless, neglectful, inactive or in derogation of their parental responsibilities provides the requisite ammunition to fight the battle against the Act and the government responsible for it. The non-residential father is able to stand up and say 'I am innocent'.[9]

The proliferation of negative discourses has created the opportunity for the production of numerous counter-discourses, discourses that are heralded as the real 'truth' of the situation, that non-residential fathers are not really 'absent' at all. Rather, they are caring, loving, contributing, active parents who happen not to reside physically with their children.[10] Once non-residential fathers have effectively demonstrated their victim status, the unfairness of the new regime of child support becomes a self-evident truth. What is more, the victimization is demonstrated as occurring on a massive scale, with huge groups of disenchanted, middle-class, male voters joining ranks against the Conservative government.

The class-based nature of the campaign against the Act is notable. Non-residential fathers have succeeded in establishing themselves as members of a large, persecuted and disillusioned group of middle-class men. And as Collier has noted, the government appears to listen to middle-class men in a way that it fails to do with other groups in society (1995a). To date, both the Conservative and the current Labour government have responded to the protest by implementing radical and substantive changes to both the Act's basic principles and its procedural rules, which in the main benefit non-residential fathers and their new families. Additionally, the current government is seeking to enhance fathers' position further in relation to children by allowing putative fathers to gain automatic parental responsibility on jointly registering the birth of a child (*The Times*, 2 February 1999: 39). Thus, it can be said that contemporary debates about

---

9. These words are taken from a demonstrator's placard. The same image was used to depict two separate instances of demonstrations against the Child Support Act in *The Guardian*: 6 April 1994 and 24 January 1995.

10. Butler 1990 describes how the possibility of agency remains ever-present in opening out alternative discursive routes or 'ways of being'.

the persistence of the father's obligations to his children are also inevitably bound up with negotiations about power. The Child Support Act can be seen as presenting a serious challenge to the gains made in men's bargaining powers on the settlement of financial matters on divorce. However, this challenge has been met by a successful counter-challenge by non-residential fathers. Moreover, recent government initiatives would seem to restate its commitment to 'the family', albeit through a reconfiguration of social policy to accommodate changing norms and values concerning the constitution of a family through cohabitation as opposed to marriage. Despite the seemingly liberal approach to 'alternative' family forms, it is not too difficult to discern the political motivation to tie men to children and to give back to men as a group some authority over the familial realm, which they might argue has been lost.

An examination of the cultural climate in which these representations are generated has been integral to my project. As demonstrated above, contemporary discourses, albeit from a number of disparate sources, have advocated the merits of father participation and correspondingly problematized father absence. Some of these discourses can be seen as attempting to respond in a sensitive way to the demands made by feminism. Others, such as those groups who advocate the reassertion of father right, can be viewed as antagonistic to the feminist project. Government debates about the Child Support Act are concerned with enforcing the non-residential father's financial responsibility for his biological children. The government attempts to justify its novel legislation by using the normative concept of continuing parental responsibility. However, due to the increased burden of child support, fathers are able to argue that their capacity for fulfilling their parental responsibilities is undermined due to economic hardship. In so doing, they are able to demonstrate that the allegations of fecklessness are false by stating that their priorities lie with the sustaining of mutually beneficial father/child relationships.

In voicing dismay, confusion and anger about the Child Support Act, men successfully establish their victim status but also furnish themselves with a basis upon which to make the claims that they have been emasculated by the state and a feminism that has gone too far. Moreover, discussion about the desirability/necessity of continuing parental responsibility, whether concerning financial, emotional or moral support, comes to revolve around how the law affects fathers. The needs of lone mothers are marginalized, and the needs of children are conflated with the wishes of their fathers. Forgotten, too, are the effects of the social and economic deprivation that many lone mothers and their children experience as a result of their lone parent family status (Hewitt and Leach 1993).

Fathers are given the opportunity to raise the debate about child support on the terms that they and their children have a right to the mutually beneficial relationship that has gained so much credence in contemporary society. It should not be forgotten that they are also seeking to re-establish some of the power that they believe has been lost due to the perceived gains in power made by women in the familial realm and by the government in assuming firm control over the issue of child support. The campaign against the Child Support Act can be seen as constituting part of a broader canvas of hostility towards the perceived inroads made by women into men's authority and control in the family. Non-residential fathers have joined with and are sometimes already allied to existing pressure groups, such as FNF and DAD. They have successfully harnessed the discourse of 'victims' in order to reclaim some of the rights that they feel they have lost as a result of women's perceived gains. It is the perceived loss of fathers' rights that precedes and permits the assertion of the 'victim' status. The campaign waged against the Act by groups of middle-class fathers has yielded a good degree of sympathy for non-residential fathers in much of the media discourse on child support. In addition, the government has responded in a benevolent way by introducing radical changes to the substantive law and the procedural rules that in the main benefit them and their new families. By establishing themselves as victims of negative and false discourses, as victims of an uncompromising and unfair law, and of a feminism that has gone too far in protecting the rights of women, non-residential fathers have secured for themselves a position of strength. It is a position that has remained untenable for lone mothers, the possible reasons for which have been stated in Chapters 2 and 3.

chapter 5

'For the sake of the children': occluding maternal desire

This chapter draws upon an empirical study of lone mothers. Before I go on to outline the details and discuss the outcome of my research, I will elucidate why I have elected to incorporate research of this kind. The chapters in this book so far bear testament to my interest in the law and other social producers of discourses that bring into being feminine (and masculine) legal and social subjects. I have shown that the lone mother is constituted in various forms by the occasional interplay and sometimes friction between the discourses that operate to constitute her as a legal and social actor. The book has also demonstrated how some discourses have a certain authority over others. In Chapter 3, I described the ways in which legal agents sometimes disqualify knowledge offered by social workers acting on behalf of the state in order to achieve an outcome based upon legal rather than psychological criteria. By so doing, the court is creating a hierarchy of authority and placing itself at the very pinnacle of that hierarchy. By centralizing and legitimizing the legal framework as the most appropriate means by which to settle familial disputes, the law at the same time sites other state institutions lower down the hierarchy. In other words, as was demonstrated in the paternal contact cases, the construction of a mother's 'implacable hostility' can be seen to be a determining and central feature in decisions about what is or, perhaps more appropriately here, what is not in a child's best interests. Choosing to refute the testimony of the psychiatric expert in one of the cases, the law claimed that it was best placed to decide upon the validity of the expert evidence. As a result, the 'expert' knowledge was found lacking by the law. Additionally, it was demonstrated how the mother's reasons for resistance to contact were either ignored or marginalized. At the same time, therefore, what is also marginalized and disqualified is the woman's experience of the situation.

The aim of this part of the research is to give voice to the subject of the lone mother, who is, as has been demonstrated, so frequently constructed as the symbol of all that is wrong with today's society. As Smart has made clear, however, the constitution of the mother in legal discourse is not simply iconographic, that is, a mere representation. For her, as for myself, discourse not only produces the subject but also produces subjectivity. According to this formulation, subjectivity is best understood as including both the social processes by which the individual is constituted and the processes by which the individual comes to recognize herself or to claim an identity (Smart 1991: 485–500). The empirical study to be discussed in this chapter has been aimed at discovering how lone mothers have come to claim an identity for themselves in the light of and also in spite of the way that they have been portrayed in legal and social discourses. Prior to the interviews, I had identified some discursive sources that had the potential to contribute to the constitution of the identities of lone mothers. My elected sources were newspaper coverage of lone mothers generally and specifically in relation to the Child Support Act, the substance of the Act itself, and newspaper coverage of what became popularly known as the 'Home Alone' cases. This included the legal construction and adjudication of one mother in particular, Heidi Colwell, who was involved in one of the cases where the law was invoked. The coverage of the Colwell story brought into being many of the important themes that came to infect social, legal and political discourses of the 1990s. I have therefore chosen to use it as a means of framing some of the main issues to be discussed here.

I have focused upon lone mothers rather than non-residential fathers because lone mothers do not seem to have been given (or taken) the opportunity to raise the debate about motherhood and child support at the level of their own everyday experiences to the extent that non-residential fathers have. In Chapter 4, it was demonstrated that non-residential fathers have succeeded in resisting the negative stereotype of 'fecklessness' by meeting the stereotype head on and inverting it to state that they are most definitely not 'feckless'. Furthermore, campaigning non-residential fathers were also successful in making a case that they were better viewed as constituting the 'victims' of an unruly state out of control. The practical implications are that fathers' campaigns contributed to bringing about reforms to the Act that benefited them and their new families. In other words, the discourses or voices of non-residential fathers have not been marginalized to the same extent as lone mothers.

Lone mothers have not used the discourses that constitute them in a negative manner as a basis for generating counter-discourses to anything like the same extent as non-residential fathers. As I suggest in Chapter 2, the closest that women appear to get to this is by rendering themselves distinct from the 'teenage' lone mother stereotype. In Chapter 4, I posited that non-residential fathers opposed to the Child Support Act consist to a large extent of a homogeneous interest group of middle-class men who stand to benefit in similar ways by the changes that they seek to bring about. Lone mothers, on the other hand, do not share a similar what I will call collective and homogeneous interest in reforming the Act. For example, those women who are fortunate enough to be independent of the state benefit system may eventually stand to gain from the new system as they will receive maintenance in addition to their own income. Under the Child Support Act's original rules, lone mothers on benefits had their maintenance deducted pound for pound from their income support (see Chapter 1 for a summary of the current Labour government's proposals for change).

Clearly, for women there is a diverse set of interests at stake in the debates over lone motherhood, 'the family' and the issue of child support. Lone mothers have not been given or taken the opportunity to raise the debate, particularly on child support, on their own terms because of the manner in which lone mothers are perceived and trumpeted as the *beneficiaries* of the Child Support Act. The interviews explored what the participants felt about the representations made of them in social and legal discourses. The study revealed how the legal and social discourses that constitute the 'problem' of lone motherhood have different effects depending on the status of the lone mother, for example her financial status, age, sexual orientation and whether she was 'single' or divorced. It has been argued that psychological and media discourses rely upon the establishment of normality rather than the exercise of coercion in the regulation of family life. According to Rose, for example:

> for the vast majority of families regulation operates by other means. Coercion plays a minor role. Family practices are increasingly aligned with social objectives not through coercion but through acting upon the wishes, desires, and aspirations of adults. Psychology has played a key role here, in establishing norms of desirable child development and behaviour, and in providing new means of visualising and understanding the nature of childhood, its normalities and pathologies. These psychological norms and languages have been disseminated not only through the education of social workers and

health visitors, but also through the terms of popular literature and
debate in the mass media, in advertising and in culture generally.

(1991: xii)

I would agree with Rose that the dispersal of normative guidelines
is widespread and pervasive and operates by acting upon the desires of
adults, who in turn regulate according to desirable and desired child
behaviours as established by psychology. These regulatory family practices
are also increasingly associated with the well-being of society. Indeed, this
book has been concerned with demonstrating how these technologies of
regulation are disseminated by discourses of the law, the academy and
the media. I have also argued that 'the family' in its traditional form is
constructed as the bedrock of society. To this extent I concur with Rose.
However, this work has also considered the ways in which *legal* discourses
have constructed the related 'problem' of child support and the concomitant 'problematic' roles of mothers and fathers. I am thus concerned
to explore how far coercion still plays a major role in the regulation of
family life despite the way that the 'law operates more and more as a norm'
(Foucault 1981: 144).

A number of aspects of the structure and operation of the Child
Support Act indicate that coercion still has a considerable impact in the
regulation of family life. For example, the legislation embraces the concept of parental responsibility as a means of justifying legislative intervention in family life. The concept is a normative one, and ongoing parental
responsibility is seen as benefiting both child(ren) and society as a whole.
Notwithstanding the normative dimension of the concept, the law seeks
to enforce the principle of responsibility by implementing punitive sanctions should cooperation with child support practices be found to be lacking. An example is section 6, where women who refuse to cooperate with
the Child Support Agency without grounds will be subject to a benefit
reduction. I argue that despite the law's employment of normative concepts such as parental responsibility, an additional element of coercion is
retained and drawn upon in order to ensure as far as is possible that the
norm is adhered to. To this extent, Rose understates the coercive aspect
of the regulation of family life, as the law not only increasingly uses normative concepts but at the same time it also brings into play mechanisms
of punishment should resistance to the norm be in evidence. To summar-
ize my position, I would agree with Rose that the regulation of families
is increasingly achieved by establishing and dispersing new norms of
behaviour, and in so doing the 'psy' disciplines, popular culture and the
media have played important roles. The law has also played an important

role as it too embraces normative guidelines in legislation governing family life. However, it has the added effect of being able to sanction mothers and fathers for failing to adhere to the normative framework and has thus the added dimension of coerciveness. The empirical study will reveal the way that lone mothers have felt threatened by the law on child support due to some of its more coercive aspects.

The book has shown how social and legal discourse has reconstituted the roles of mothers and fathers by drawing upon academic disciplines and political and social discourses around the contemporary role of the family. In Chapter 2, I showed how the Conservative government represented lone mothers in their worst possible light and as a major problem that needed resolving. It is clear, however, that women's experiences as lone mothers are diverse and are likely to vary according to class, ethnicity, sexual affiliation and position in the labour market. Diversity notwithstanding, this small study also revealed many similarities among the participants' experiences of living in lone mother headed households. Perhaps one of the most obvious similarities is that they are linked by a mutual concern to do their best for their children. This study seeks to enable a small number of lone mothers to be heard in the midst of recent vituperative attacks. The participating mothers tell stories about life with their children, how they cope with practical constraints such as lack of adequate resources, how the new legislation has impacted upon their lives and about how the negative representations made of them affect their selfhood. Several key themes will be explored in the chapter. I will consider the impact of media discourses upon the participating lone mothers, how mothers cope with poverty and the problems associated with the lone parent household gaining financial autonomy. I will also pursue the theme of the relationship between the selfhood of the lone mother and her child(ren).

The study

During a period between June 1994 and September 1995, I interviewed nine women about their experiences as lone mothers. This small sample is therefore intended to be illustrative rather than representative of the lives of lone mothers as a social group. In other words, my concern is to aid in the story telling of the women in the study. The study is intended to show how these women make sense of their lives as lone mothers through the network of discourses that contribute to their sense of self. It is also concerned to show the agency of lone mothers in engaging in and in constituting their subject identity as lone mother. The women were contacted in one of several ways. Two of the participants responded to an advertisement placed in *The Guardian* in June 1994, which called for lone mothers who had experience of the Child Support Agency. One of the participants responded to the same advertisement placed in the lesbian publication *Shebang* in the same month. I also asked *Woman* and *Woman's Own* to run the advertisement for me, but they refused. It was my intention to attract as wide a cross-section of lone mothers as possible (given the limits of time and financial resources) in an attempt to explore women's differences of experience based upon class, sexual affiliation and ethnicity. In early 1995, I placed a further advertisement in the local newspaper and as a result two more women came forward to volunteer to participate in the project. Later that year, I contacted a branch of *Gingerbread*, the lone parents' support group, which put me in touch with a former member willing to contribute to the project. My association with the *Gingerbread* group led me to another group in Cumbria. After a visit to that group, two more women volunteered to participate. The remaining participant was alerted to the work in progress by one of my own personal friends.

The women involved in the study were either in their twenties, thirties or forties. Five of the participants had only one child each. One of the participants had three children, another had twins and two of the participants had two children each. All of the women had been lone mothers for at least eighteen months at the time of the initial interview. The longest period that had been spent as a lone mother was eleven years. The children were aged between three and twenty. The interviews were open-ended, but I did have a sketched outline of issues that I wanted to discuss with each of the participants. The outline was in effect a list of matters to be covered. The list included the woman's work situation, income support, the Child Support Act and how the participants felt about popular and legal representations of lone mothers. The overall aim of the interviews was to discern how women made sense of their lives as lone mothers. I wanted to consider the structural facets of their lives: for example, how they experienced the financial aspects of being in a lone mother headed household. I also wanted to investigate how they experienced their lives at the emotional level.

Notwithstanding the use of a standardized list of topics to be covered with the participants, discussions were largely unstructured. For example, the order in which the issues were covered was very much guided and determined by the participants. When questions were necessary (very often the participants contributed so fully that they guided me from one topic to another) they were open-ended in an attempt to maximize the description of the participants' life experiences. The use of the open-ended interview proved particularly valuable in revealing similarities and differences between the participants.

As the research progressed, it became very clear that the women had been located in very different social positions before they became lone mothers, for example some identifying as middle-class and others as working-class. However, the assumption of the lone mother status did seem to be sufficient to provide the women with a means by which they could identify with other lone mothers. The identification of lone mothers with other lone mothers often arose in the conversations about their negative representation in media discourses. There was a strong sense that the participants wanted to refute the stereotype of the 'feckless' lone mother on behalf of themselves and other lone mothers. I acknowledge that this might appear to contradict my earlier claim in Chapter 2 that for women there is a diverse set of interests at stake in debates over child support. However, I would argue that those discourses that have the effect of denigrating lone mothers raise a different set of interests than do debates about child support. For example, child support involves the consideration of women's financial interests, which may be diversely affected by the Act, depending upon whether women have independent means or rely on state benefits. Debates about lone motherhood, on the other hand, and especially negative representations of lone mothers, call into question the integrity of women as mothers, which there might be a collective interest in protecting.

The unstructured nature of the discussions also proved useful for generating new themes or ideas. For example, in one of the discussions a participant made a distinction between women who parent alone during periods of war and women who parent alone because of divorce or widowhood. The distinction was used to draw my attention to the stigma that many of the participants feel is attached to them purely on the basis of their status as divorced or never-married lone mothers. It was thought that no such stigma had been attached to women who parent alone during times of war. Moreover, the comment was also indicative of the manner in which lone mothers explore their own social standing by comparing and contrasting popular discourses in particular social and historical contexts. The avoidance of a rigidly structured interview programme enabled the women to contribute to the research agenda.

Because of the unstructured nature of the interviews, they could last anything from one to three hours, sometimes with the promise of food at the end. In all of the cases, I was welcomed heartily by participants.

Their generosity was not quashed by the frequent lack of adequate financial resources. I was also often surprised at the ease with which the women spoke about their lives, even when they had suffered in a physical or emotional way. I felt that they were as responsible as myself for generating an atmosphere that was conducive to the discussion of issues that can only be described as intimate parts of their lives. In this I am grateful not only for their actual verbal contributions to the project but also for their generosity of spirit, which is impossible to capture and demonstrate fully on paper.

My reading of the legal and social discourses about lone motherhood has not been concerned to show the truth or falsity of the representations. The idea that representations of mothers can be either true or false rests upon the predicate that there is an authentic self that exists as pure, unmediated and beyond representation. Rather, I argue that all the stories about lone mothers and their children, including the stories that women tell for themselves, are mediated and linked to other social discourses. So, for example, the way in which the participants make sense of their lives is linked to the manner in which they are represented in other discourses. At the same time, what is said in discourses about lone motherhood is inevitably linked to what is known (Lawler 1995: 37). Discursive representations of lone mothers draw upon what is known about lone mothers. For example, the pejorative nature of the representation of women who wilfully parent alone is influenced by sets of ideas that have been developed to show that children benefit from having a man in their lives. The women who participated in this project are using social stories and legal discourse in order to make sense of and define their own lives. This research does not suggest that the women's stories are authentic while the media stories are false, misrepresentations or incomplete realities that only need supplementing to get the whole of the picture. Rather, I am concerned with examining the manner in which the women's stories are linked to the social discourses about them and how these discourses impact upon the women's lives. First, I will outline the socio-political context in which the Colwell case arose and reveal the significance of the story of Heidi Colwell for the discussion of the empirical research that follows.

Trying mother: the case of Heidi Colwell

As was shown in Chapter 2, the social and political climate in the early to mid-1990s saw lone mothers subjected to a great deal of vilification in the press coverage of the new law on child support, in discussions about 'the family' and in debates about lone motherhood. Like Lochhead's 'Mother' at the start of Chapter 1, the lone mother of contemporary discourse is relied on to fulfil her children's needs in the face of the non-presence of the father. Mothers therefore become defined through an articulation of the needs of their children. However, lone mothers face particular difficulties in meeting these needs. I will later argue that in debates about what children need there is no accompanying discussion of the needs of the mother. A lone mother's needs become occluded by the needs of her children. Heidi Colwell was a lone mother who elected to go out to work rather than rely on state benefits. Her two-year-old daughter was left alone at home while Colwell worked to support them both. A concerned neighbour reported the situation to Social Services.

The press response to the Colwell case ranged from incredulity to a surprisingly supportive stance from the *Daily Telegraph*. The *Daily Telegraph* suggested that Heidi would probably have been financially better off relying on state support, estimating a likely sum of £101 per week. At the time of the incident, Colwell was earning £100 per week, and she said in defence of her actions that she could not afford to pay a child minder. Additionally, the *Daily Telegraph* claimed that prior to securing employment and the council house that she then inhabited, she had lived in 'appalling council bed and breakfast accommodation' (3 August 1993). The *Daily Telegraph* also made much of the fact that Colwell had sought to establish her independence from social security provision, remarking that she 'did not want to throw herself on the mercy of the state' (*ibid*.). Lynda Lee Potter wrote in the *Daily Mail* (4 August 1993): 'I don't feel anger for the child's mother so much as disbelief and an utter lack of comprehension.' *The Times* (20 August 1993) stressed that Colwell had been abandoned by her partner rather than choosing to parent alone.

Colwell initially received a six-month prison sentence after admitting charges of cruelty by ill-treating, neglecting and abandoning her daughter.[1] The Court of Appeal later reduced the sentence and she was freed and placed on two years probation after she had served seventeen days of her prison sentence. It was reported in *The Times* (20 August 1993) that the Court of Appeal had ruled that the original trial judge had failed to balance the need to impose a prison sentence against the needs of the child. While the higher court maintained that a prison sentence had been the correct measure, it regarded the length of sentence as too severe and that it was not in the best interests of her child. It was reported in *The Guardian* (20 August 1993) that a non-custodial sentence would have

---

1. s. 1(1) of the Children and Young Person's Act 1933.

'risked sending the wrong signals to parents tempted to leave very young children for long periods of time'. The case also prompted a number of sympathetic responses from a variety of support groups. Nikki Jones of the National Council for One Parent Families was quoted in the *Daily Telegraph* as saying:

> It's unrealistic to expect people to make the leap from low but secure income support to the higher-paid but riskier world of work without any support to cover child care.   (4 August 1993)

Sally Witcher of the Child Poverty Action Group claimed:

> The Government is currently reviewing social security expenditure. Improving child care provision would be a constructive way of decreasing benefits expenditure.   (*The Guardian*, 28 August 1993)

Similar comments were made by other groups, including the Working Mothers' Association, Working for Childcare. The urgent need for childcare support for lone parents wanting to work was emphasized, and much of the press took a sympathetic approach to Colwell's case. *The Guardian* published several letters written by the general public that expressed outrage at the judgement of the court of first instance (5 August 1993).

Even the traditionally right-wing papers spoke in support of Colwell. The Appeal Court also demonstrated some sympathy for Colwell's actions. Lord Justice Steyn, who presided over the case, stated that the original trial judge had failed to balance the circumstances that gave rise to Colwell's actions and the impact of the prison sentence on the child against the need to protect children from neglect (*The Times*, 29 August 1993). He also stated that Colwell had made:

> strenuous efforts to solve her problems; she had asked about council nurseries and applied for council housing . . . she received no further help . . . Jessica was otherwise well looked after and her mother never left her in the evenings or at weekends.   (*Daily Mail*, 20 August 1993)

The newspaper reports of the Colwell case extolled her behaviour through the employment of a conglomeration of images: first, her *efforts* to improve her and her child's lives by establishing independence from the state benefit system, electing instead to seek paid employment; second, her *struggle* to overcome the *appalling* conditions of her life; third, another relevant theme was the representation of her *attachment* to her maternal work when she was not out at her job but at home with her daughter. In short, her life would seem to be dedicated to work. In none of the media coverage I examined was Colwell represented as deriving any *pleasure* outside the sphere of her maternal work. Even though she opted to work outside the home, the decision to do so and leave her daughter alone was represented as driven by her desire to provide her child with improved living conditions. Her only pleasure was constructed as deriving from her maternal duties.

The *Daily Mail* recounted Colwell's motivations as given in her statement to the police:

> I got my priorities wrong. It was a question of having a good income and a good life or going back to bed and breakfast and income support. If I'd had enough money it wouldn't have been a problem. But it was a choice of paying the bills and having decent food and clothes, not just from jumble sales, or having a childminder and bringing Jessica to a cold house with bread and milk. I did it the best way I could.   (20 August 1993)

The Independent cited Colwell thus:

> It was a choice between food and clothes and a childminder. I don't know if I thought about the risk. I suppose I put it to the back of my mind . . . It was a case of that or not keeping my job and living on benefit.   (3 August 1993)

There is a startling paradox in the messages emitted from the array of sympathetic responses to the Colwell case. On the one hand, Colwell was applauded for her strenuous efforts to provide for her child through employment rather than rely on the state for support. On the other hand, she received a custodial sentence designed to sanction her failure to provide an adequate standard of care for her daughter. The case highlights the problems faced by many lone mothers who want/need to return to work. Childcare is expensive. There is at the same time a strong political commitment to cut down on public expenditure. However, recent changes offer potential improvements to aid lone mothers' transition into paid employment. The Child Support Act 1995 introduced a new scheme whereby the parent with care in receipt of income support can build up credits of £5 per week towards a maximum of £1,000 which can be redeemed on gaining employment over sixteen hours a week.[2] In 1998, the Labour government announced its national child care strategy and in the March 1998 budget introduced the working families tax credit, which includes a component for childcare. The childcare tax credit is intended to meet 70 per cent of eligible childcare costs up to £100 per week for one child and £150 per week for two or more children. It came into effect in October 1999.

---

2.   Social Security (Child Maintenance *Bonus*) Regs. SI 1996/3195.

As has been noted by Diduck and Kaganas, the Labour government has also committed itself to providing day care (or school) places for all four-year-olds but has not stated when or how this is to happen (1999: 92).

The former Conservative government singled out lone mothers as a reason for the high rate of public expenditure. The current government sees the solution as encouraging lone mothers into employment through in-work incentives. However, Finlayson and Marsh have noted the problems associated with this strategy. They claim that the government is not just supplementing low wages but also low-skill, part-time employment, which is detrimental to long-term career patterns. When lone parents' children become self-sufficient, it is likely that their parents will still be in low-paid employment (Finlayson and Marsh 1998: 204). It is also claimed that the stigma associated with such benefits acts as a deterrent to the eligible claiming them in the first place (ibid.). Lone mothers like Heidi sometimes seek to escape the stigma that is associated with being dependent upon state benefits. They may at the same time also feel torn between their caring obligations and their need to secure extra income. As Edwards and Duncan state: 'Some lone mothers may give primacy to the moral benefit of physically caring for their children themselves over the financial benefits of undertaking paid employment' (1996: 120).

Although the two aspects of care are linked, they are not necessarily always compatible and women may face difficult choices. If women choose to remain on state benefit, they are likely to be berated for their actions and forced to live in impoverished conditions. If they are successful in obtaining employment outside the home, then they will need to secure sufficient remuneration to be able to afford childcare. If a lone mother succeeds on all these counts, she still has to ensure that her child is well cared for at all times. As any lone mother knows, her maternal work is boundless. She will provide her children with a stream of practical support, including food, clothing and warmth. Additionally, she may have sole responsibility for checking homework, and for transport to doctors, dentists and physical care when the child is ill. There will also be a need to provide the emotional support and moral guidance necessary to enable the child to make the transition into adult life. As demonstrated in Chapter 2, the lone mother's ability to fulfil this function has come under strident attack recently (see, for example, Dennis and Erdos 1992, whose work was used by Peter Lilley in his 1993 Conservative Party Conference speech).

The Colwell case has been used as an example to show the potential problems that may be faced by lone mothers who want to provide financially for their children rather than relying on the state benefit system. Women need to find well-paid employment in order to meet childcare costs. However, the evidence suggests that women are still economically disadvantaged in the labour market (Lister 1989). A depressed market offering poorly remunerated work with little job security tempers the likelihood of securing well-paid employment. Women are often forced to rely upon the unpaid care of other women. The Colwell case stands as a stark reminder of the difficulties of mothers combining the two aspects of care for a child, that is in a financial sense and in the sense of providing day-to-day care physical and emotional care. Colwell was constructed in the press discourses as a woman struggling to gain her independence from the state. Indeed, Colwell stated that her choice to work and leave her child alone was preferable to relying on state benefits. She received a good deal of sympathy from social and legal commentators precisely because of her efforts to support her child financially. However, there is a paradox in the signals transmitted by the responses. On the one hand, Colwell was applauded for her efforts to provide financially for her daughter, but on the other hand, she failed to meet the day-to-day care needed by her daughter and was legally sanctioned for that failure. However, what is clear is that Colwell's role was defined through a discourse of meeting the needs of her daughter. At this point, I turn to the relevance of needs discourse to debates about mothering more generally.

The desire to work of the participants in this study was often driven by the perception that work is the only means by which women can secure the financial independence of the family. The need to secure the autonomy of the family in the post-separation context relies very much on the desire to provide a better life for the children. The participants in this study highlighted the obstacles faced by lone mothers seeking employment. Women face difficult choices because of the way the two aspects of financial and practical care are linked. While the two elements of providing financially for the child and providing her/him with an adequate standard of care are related, there can be problems trying to combine the two aspects of caring. A predominant theme in the study was that the women strove to cope and frequently sacrificed their own needs/desires for the sake of the children.

The significance of 'needs' discourse

The duty of mothers to care for their children is articulated through a discourse of the child's needs. For example, in the government's White Paper on the Child Support Act 1991 (HMSO 1990), the justification for

the inclusion of a 'parent as carer' allowance in the formula for the maintenance requirement is stated thus:

> A child needs not only to be fed and clothed. He also needs someone
> to look after him. An adult who has to care for children has more
> limited choices about how far she can travel for employment, or
> how many hours she can work. She may not be able to work at all,
> especially when the children are very young. These are costs incurred
> by the adult because of the child's need for care and so are part of the
> costs of caring for the child.
>
> (cited in Wages for Housework and Payday men's network: 1993)

The adult who cares for the child will almost always be a woman.
This is recognized by the Child Support Act through the use of the female
personal pronoun when referring to the 'parent with care'. The 'child' of
the legislation is represented by the male pronoun, which is usually used
in statutes. Therefore, it is the mother who usually meets the child's needs
as articulated above. The passage emphasizes the expectation that maternal practices will meet the child(ren)'s needs. The White Paper acknowledges on the one hand the care that mothers are responsible for while
on the other hand denying mothering any real status as work by stating
later in the passage that women may not be able to work at all. The child
is constructed as having needs that have to be met by someone. The
law rightly assumes that usually the mother will meet the child's day-to-
day needs. The mother has a duty to fulfil the needs of her child, and the
meeting of those needs might mean that the mother is unable to gain
employment outside her maternal role. Nowhere in the above statement
is there any mention that the mother might also have needs of her own.

In the case of the 'parent as carer' allowance, it is the father who
is required to pay for her maternal practices whenever possible as it is
calculated as part of his maintenance assessment in an attempt by the
government to shift responsibility for the family back onto itself. What
is ignored in this is the benefit that accrues to society as a whole as a
result of women's caring activities. There is no sense of a communal
responsibility owed to children. If neither man nor state is willing to provide adequate remuneration for the child's needs then who is left with
the responsibility but the mother? The idea that it is mothers who are
responsible for the day-to-day care and nurturing of children remains
prevalent in discourses on child support. Messages about whether or not
women should seek employment outside the home in order to care for
their child(ren) are less transparent because of the manner in which a
mother's role still remains defined through her day-to-day care obligations.

With regard to the lone mother, these maternal obligations to fulfil her children's needs may also involve her being the main source of financial support for the children. If the mother's role is articulated through the needs of her children, what then happens to her own needs or desires?

Stephanie Lawler has highlighted the manner in which discourses about children's needs are inextricably linked to the mother's competing needs, although they are not explicitly considered in needs discussions (1995: 264). She further argues that when mothers do allude to their own potential needs claims, those claims are frequently occluded by those of the child. This closure of the woman's needs is achieved in two movements: by the invocation of a 'congruence of needs between mother and child'; and by the 'translation of claims of maternal "need" into maternal desires' (*ibid.*: 270). The first movement incorporates the construction of the mother's needs as being the same as the child's. The second movement involves a translation of women's needs claims to those of 'desires'. She argues that women's needs, once translated into desires, can be constructed as little more than 'dangerous selfishness', while greater legitimacy will be attributed to children's needs (*ibid.*).

In Chapter 3, I demonstrated how cases concerning paternal contact claims are resolved through the concept of the best interests of the child. I showed that there is a strong judicial tendency towards the idea that children need fathers. Women who seek to keep the father from the child are constructed as acting upon a wilful desire, even though there might be evidence of some need to keep the father away from the child. At the same time, the mothers involved in the cases are constructed as wilful and dangerous. More importance is always ascribed to the child's needs than to the constructed desires of the mother to keep the man from the child. According to Woodhead (1990), the lack of value ascribed to desire is a consequence of the way in which desire may or may not be met with little impact either way. Needs, on the other hand, must be met or dire consequences may follow.

It is notable that popular discourses on working lone mothers often emphasize the need for lone mothers to work in order to provide for their children. Rarely do these discourses speak of a lone mother's need to work for personal fulfilment. However, when there is a parental dispute over the residence of children, women who are constructed as working in order to fulfil their own personal needs are subjected to judicial disapproval. Graycar cites an Australian example of judicial disapprobation of the mother's 'tendency to allow herself to be so absorbed by her personal ambitions as to show a lack of maternal feelings towards the children and to be unconscious of and unsympathetic to their emotional needs'

(1989: 76).[3] O'Donovan uses the above example to demonstrate how a full-time working mother is perceived by the law as lacking the 'qualifications of a "real mother"' (1993: 76).

In other words, 'real mothers' place their child's needs above their own. Indeed, real mothers define their own needs as being the same as their children's. The Colwell case was viewed in a sympathetic way *because* her drive to work was constructed as being motivated by a concern to provide a better life for her child. The example taken from Graycar suggests that mothers are regarded as being incapable of fulfilling their own need to work and of meeting their children's needs. The lone mother has to strive with competing sets of discourses that valorize the autonomous mother while defining a mother's role as primarily concerned with the day-to-day practical and emotional care of her children. Moreover, in performing this task not any standard of care will suffice. A mother has to fulfil a certain set of criteria in order to show herself to be a good mother. She must be sensitive to all her children's needs and be selfless in her role as a mother.[4]

Lone mothers can thus meet their own personal aspirations only by ensuring first and foremost that the happiness and well-being of their children are secured. Rose makes the point thus:

> The family now will meet its social obligations through promising to meet the personal aspirations of its members, as adults construe the maximisation of the physical and mental welfare of their offspring as the privileged path to their own happiness.   (1992: 156–7)

Rose's analysis is useful in so far as it outlines how families regulate themselves through the fulfilment of personal desires. According to Rose, adult family members align their own personal aspirations with the happiness of their children. However, the above statement is problematic because of the way that it speaks of 'the family' as if there was only one family form. In other words, Rose fails to address the very particular difficulties that might arise for marginalized family forms. For example, lone mothers are subjected to extreme forms of pressure in attaining their social and personal obligations, which are defined within a set of discourses about the idealized family. Lone mothers do seek to secure the happiness of their children and to produce normal, healthy children, thus fulfilling their

---

3. Quote taken from the case of Harrington *v.* Hynes [1982] 8 Family Law Reports (Australia) 295–376 and used in Graycar 1989. Also cited in O'Donovan 1993.

4. For a discussion of the 'sensitive' mother, see Walkerdine and Lucey 1989: 57–63. Also, Rose 1989: 200–9.

social obligation. They can be subjected to extreme forms of pressure that might not be encountered by the traditional family. They may have severe financial difficulties, as earning potential is often restricted to one person, and at the same time they may have the added problem of renegotiating fractured familial relationships with their estranged partners for the sake of their children. What I found striking about all the participants' transcripts was the way that lone mothers aligned their own interests very much with their children's. This appeared to be the case with Martha, who stated:

> I have to go out to work and I have to find work quick because I just can't manage. If I do go back to work I have to earn £200 per week net. £200 would be top wages as a daily nanny. I'd be working from 9 o'clock (because I couldn't work any earlier) straight through till 7 o'clock. I'll be working flat out all those hours and then have to come back and deal with my own children as well. All it means is at the end of the month I'll have £100 for food and £60 left over for shoes. They all need new shoes.

She later added:

> I'd rather spend John's nursery years with him but the CSA won't let me. He will have to go to work with me and watch me look after other children. I'm damn good at what I do . . . I want to go back to work . . . What about childcare for people like me who have to go out to work? I have to find childcare. If I'm employed as a daily nanny it means paying someone to look after my kids after school. It's not going to be worth it . . . I'm in a Catch 22 situation.

At some points, she states that she 'wants' to return to her career as a nanny because she is good at it and at other points she stresses a 'need' to work to provide financially for her family. Furthermore, she notes a conflict between wanting to spend her time with John, her youngest child, during his nursery years and needing to return to work so that she can support all her children.

Martha's comments are indicative of the problems faced by lone mothers who need or want to return to work. Affordable childcare is in short supply, as are jobs that provide an income capable of raising women above the income support level. Martha's need to work is defined in terms of her wanting to work at something that she is good at. On the one hand, Martha aligns her need to work with the practical activity of providing financially for her children. On the other hand, there is a desire to do something that she is good at – look after children. Her decision as to whether or not to work is justified in terms of wanting to provide for her family. She defines her need to work as a 'want' and maps that desire onto her attempts to meet her children's needs. There may be a desire on the part of the mother to work for her own pleasure, but that desire is occluded by her desire to fulfil the needs of her children. She articulates a conflict between wanting to spend her son's early years with him and wanting to go out to work. The only way that she can earn enough to provide adequately for her family is by working long hours.

Her choices are attenuated by structural factors and also by her feelings of guilt about needing to work at the expense of providing her own personal care for her son. Martha's ambiguity about work might be partly explained by the mixed messages that are transmitted about whether or not women with children should work. Beck has noted how with the breakdown of 'the family' women face new strains through attempting to reconcile contradictions involving traditional gender roles and newly assigned roles:

> the lives of women are pulled back and forth by this contradiction between liberation from and reconnection to the old ascribed roles . . . They flee from housework to a career and back again, and attempt in different phases of their lives to hold together the diverging conditions of their life 'somehow' through contradictory decisions.
>
> (Beck 1992: 111–12, cited in Smart and Neale 1999: 13)

Beck succinctly states the problems facing women attempting to reconcile the 'pull of tradition and the push of modernity' (Smart and Neale 1999: 13). His analysis is useful for understanding the complex issues involved in lone mothers' decisions as to whether or not to work outside the home. On the one hand, Martha is attracted by the idea of providing day-to-day care for her son. On the other hand, she notes the appeal of pursuing her career as a nanny.

Martha's ambivalence towards paid employment might also be explained by the conflict she experiences as a result of acknowledging her own 'need' to work. The mother's role is articulated through a discourse of her children's needs. In the case of the lone mother, her role may consist of both providing financially for the child (in the absence of a male or female provider or a state willing to provide) and providing an adequate standard of care. She may find that she faces a specific kind of intense pressure that the partnered mother does not encounter. The two aspects of providing for a child financially and day-to-day care are linked. Problems therefore arise when there is a disjuncture between them.

For Martha, it is important to have a working role that is independent of the caring role that she plays in her own family's life in order to fulfil some of her own personal needs. It is notable that popular discourses on working lone mothers often emphasize the need for lone mothers to work in order to provide for their children. Rarely do these discourses speak of a lone mother's need to work for personal fulfilment. The lone mother has to strive with competing sets of discourses, which both valorise the autonomous mother and define a mother's role as primarily concerned with the day-to-day practical and emotional care of her children. These competing discourses help to explain the conflict that Martha has about her wanting to work in order to fulfil her own needs and wanting to fulfil her maternal care obligations. Martha noted the difficulties of going back to work, including long working hours (perhaps leading to physical and emotional strain when she comes to care for her own children). She would also have to earn a substantial sum of money in order to be able to deal with the extra expenses incurred as a result of her employment. Martha worries about the impact of the potential difficulties upon herself and her children. For Martha, as for the other mothers who stated a desire to work, that desire was in the main overshadowed by the need to provide adequate care for their children. In other words, the mothers' personal desires are sometimes occluded by the needs of their children. This was the case whether the women worked or not. Some of the participants defined their desire in terms of meeting the needs of their children.

Eight of the nine participants had claimed income support at some stage after the end of their relationships. Mavis, at the time of the interview, was in receipt of state benefits in order to support herself and her daughter. She had been a lone mother for seven years. Her daughter was one year old at the time of the separation from her partner. She had never received any maintenance from her daughter's father and had been in receipt of income support during her time alone with her child. When I asked how she coped financially on income support, she responded thus:

> It's very hard – you have to do without. Obviously if your daughter needs something and you're wanting to go out your daughter wins, every time. You just – it's Peter and Paul every time you're always robbing one to pay the other, and you just hope that nothing drastic happens anything financial because I just don't, if anything happened, I don't know where I would get the money from.

Clearly, Mavis finds it very difficult to manage on her state benefits. Her dependence upon these benefits places her and her daughter in a financially precarious position. The inference from Mavis' statement is that she manages to survive on her income support as long as nothing unusual happens to put a strain on her already limited resources. Moreover, Mavis highlights the manner in which she prioritizes her daughter's needs over her own when money is tight. She copes with the lack of adequate finances by sacrificing her own potential personal pleasure of going out. The strategies that Mavis adopts in order to cope with inadequate financial resources are shaped by her responsibilities to her child. The distribution of the family's income indicates the way in which women will put the needs of their children first. By impoverishing themselves, women will help to prevent or reduce the poverty of their children (Lewis and Piachaud 1992). Studies have also indicated that women will sacrifice their own personal allocation of food rather than cut down the family's collective consumption (Graham 1987: 71). Thus, a woman can enrich her child's life while impoverishing her own.

Mavis' existence is very much defined by her responsibilities to meet her child's needs. She articulates her own need for a break as a 'want' rather than a need. As I argue above, desires are seen as having less validity than needs. Mavis simply and straightforwardly occludes her own desire to go out so that she can meet her daughter's needs. Lawler's empirical study of the mother/daughter relationship showed that putting the needs of the child first was regarded by her participating mothers as characteristic of the 'good mother'. She notes that 'only one desire – the desire to be the good mother – could claim any legitimacy when faced with children's needs' (Lawler 1995: 271). When women's needs can be constructed as conflicting with the needs of their children, women's actions are led by the desire to do right by their children. When I asked Mavis where she saw her future, she replied:

> I'd go back to work tomorrow [she adds in response to my question as to what the problems are in getting back to work] . . . The problems are, it's fitting your work in with childcare. I mean, I'm lucky because I've got my mother but I'm not always going to have my mother. Childcare is expensive and in Borlston it's rare [Borlston is a fictional town].

Her maternal work of caring for her child very much shapes her lifestyle with regard to her social life and her employment pattern (Oppenheim and Harker 1996: 98). According to previously conducted research, the majority of lone mothers state a desire to return to work (NCOPF 1990). All of the participants in this study stated an intention to work outside the home. The lack of affordable childcare is recognized as one barrier to women's employment outside the home. Lone mothers like Mavis may seek to escape the stigma that is associated with being dependent on state benefits. They may also feel torn between their caring obligations and their need to secure extra income.

During the mid-1990s, it became clear that the Child Support Act had failed to ensure that non-resident fathers paid for the support of their children. Keen to retract further the role of the state, the Labour government announced that after April 1998 no new claims for one-parent benefit would be accepted, and those new claimants of income support would not qualify for the one-parent premium (see further, Lewis 1998: 251–83). In effect, social policy now focuses on helping lone mothers into work. This has led to difficult questions as to whether lone mothers should be expected to take paid employment rather than stay at home and care for their children (Millar 1994: 29). It also forces women to weigh the demands of their families against the need to provide financial security through the labour market. What this and other studies show is that women, when making a decision as to whether to work or not, rationalize their decisions based on a balancing exercise between financial and non-financial gains (see, for example, Ford 1998: 208–25). Mavis highlighted that women need to find affordable, reliable childcare. Women need to find well-paid employment in order to meet childcare costs. However, the evidence suggests that women are still economically disadvantaged in the labour market (Lister 1992). In effect, lone mothers who seek to gain paid employment are required to hand over hands-on care to another woman, sometimes at a substantial financial cost. The lone mothers in this study found the balance between providing financially and direct childcare to be complex. The difficulty of combining the two aspects of care was also highlighted in the discussions with my participants. Martha's description of being 'in a Catch 22 situation' was typical of lone mothers' experiences (for other examples, see Ford 1998: 216; Edwards and Duncan 1996: 120). Additionally, the participants wanted to come off state benefits.

Seven out of the nine women I spoke to had embarked upon some form of retraining since they had become lone mothers, with the purpose of securing full-time employment. The remaining two participants had had careers before having their children. They all hoped to return to work at some point. Alicia, who was a teacher before she had her children, recounted her strenuous efforts to secure steady employment:

> Well, I've tried very hard to get a proper job. I've applied for
> everything I could with absolutely no response. Except the classroom
> assistant job at the local comprehensive, they said I'd interviewed well
> but that I was over-qualified and would I come in as a supply teacher?
> That was good because it boosted up my self-confidence. I'm not just
> someone living on benefits anymore.

Alicia attempts to make the most of her existing skills as a teacher. The supply teaching she manages to secure fails to provide the steady income that she desperately needs. However, she is given an emotional boost by the job offer. Moreover, she states that as a result of the job she was no longer 'just someone living on benefits'. It occurred to me that although previous research had revealed that the majority of lone mothers wanted to return to work, it tended to focus solely upon the obstacles that operated against lone mothers who wanted to return to the employment market (Joshi 1990). Scant attention has been paid to why lone mothers seek to re-enter employment. I was interested in speaking to the women about their motivations for returning to work. Were they driven purely by economic necessity, or were their decisions informed by some other rationale?

I believe that Alicia's comment that the newly found position as a supply teacher meant that she was no longer 'just someone living on benefits' gives a clue to why women feel they must return to work. I decided to ask participants about how they felt about being dependent on state benefits. When I asked Alicia how she felt about claiming state benefits, she replied:

> Well it was very embarrassing really, and I was so naive I didn't even know what income support was. I must have been desperate, absolutely desperate. I really was in a very bad state. It was a very bad stigma because it clashed with the time that all the tabloids were talking about single mums and income support, and there I was in the village where my parents lived, on income support.

Like some of the other participants Alicia noted the difficulty of securing regular, affordable childcare. She relies on her own mother to substitute for her on occasions such as sports days and in the main is forced to rely on friends and neighbours to care for her child if and when she has some supply teaching. She cannot afford formal childcare. She wants to be more than someone 'on income support'.

Amy had never cohabited with or been married to her son's father. They had known each other for years, had been at school together and had met each other again when Amy was about twenty-nine. The pregnancy occurred about five months into their relationship and was unplanned. Isaac, the child's father, had wanted Amy to terminate the pregnancy, but she refused.

Before the Child Support Agency took over the administration of maintenance, Isaac had been ordered to pay £100 per month by the courts. He paid the due amount after the court had established paternity. Amy then decided to improve her education in order to start a new career. When I asked Amy about her motivation for going back to college, she replied:

> I don't like being a burden on the state . . . I like having a job and
> I like having my own income. And I also like having the freedom
> to choose what I do with my own life – whether I go on holiday,
> whether I buy a new car, whether I do the house up. You have so
> much more independence in your own life. You have choices you can
> make for yourself. Whereas when you're on income support you don't
> have any choice other than exist, and it is exist. There is absolutely
> no money left over to do anything, to give any value to your child's
> life or to enhance it in any way.

It would appear from Amy's opening line that she has to some extent internalized the view that lone mothers in receipt of state benefits are a 'burden' on the state. Additionally, however, Amy refers to the way that employment has the potential to provide the wage earner with greater lifestyle choices. It is notable that she not only refers to her own personal freedom but also closely associates the idea of having money with the means by which she can enrich her child's life. Here, Amy is giving priority to the financial benefits of undertaking paid employment and also to the idea that it is morally better to be financially independent of the state. Unlike Martha, Amy has no dilemma between the need to provide hands-on care and the need to provide financial independence. As Edwards and Duncan argue, the choice between the two will depend on the common norms shared by their social group and local social network. They further claim that lone mothers' individual calculations need to be placed in the 'framework of gendered moral rationalities that are constructed, negotiated and sustained socially in particular contexts' (Edwards and Duncan 1996: 120–1). By attempting to make sense of women's decisions over whether or not to work in a contextually specific framework, the room for marginalization of lone mothers as a group is contracted. The Labour government's proposals for in-work benefits may go some way to assisting lone mothers into employment, but as has been noted above, the movement into work may not be without its own problems. Moreover, by insisting that paid employment is the route out of poverty, women whose choice is guided by a concern to provide direct care for their children may be further marginalized because of their election to stay at home. While there may be areas of commonality between lone mothers as a social group, generalizations about women 'being wedded' to the state lead to a pernicious representation of lone mothers as irresponsible and feckless. Lone mothers who are dependent on the state for support should not be forced to deal with discourses that render them as 'welfare scroungers'.

Lone mothers internalize the view that the way to meet their own personal aspirations is through ensuring first and foremost the happiness and well-being of their children. Escape from state dependency is trumpeted as one of the main ways in which to meet the needs of lone mothers' families.

Rose argues that the successful incorporation of these constructed norms of behaviour into modern private families means that the need for government by coercion is reduced (1992: 156–7). He states:

> The modern private family remains intensively governed, it is linked in so many ways with social, economic and political objectives. But government here acts not through mechanisms of social control and subordination of the will, but through the promotion of subjectivities, the construction of pleasures and ambitions, and the activation of guilt, anxiety, envy and disappointment. The new relational technologies of the family are installed within us.   (*ibid.*)

Rose's statement has strong resonances for the modern, traditional middle-class family, which can be constructed as conforming to the promotion of normative behaviours. However, the interviews in my study indicate that the family that is constructed as falling outside the norm and therefore also as failing to inculcate the desired norms of behaviour, in other words not self-regulating, will still be subjected to coercive practices.

At this point, it is pertinent to show how the Child Support Agency employs both the coercive aspects of social control and the normalizing techniques of the activation of guilt, anxiety and shame in seeking to ensure that responsibility for the financial support of children remains with the biological family. When families can be constructed as failing to self-regulate according to accepted normative behaviours, then guilt, anxiety and coercive threat are all available to those responsible for policing the area of child support. Martha states how she feels that the Child Support Agency prevents her looking after her young son. While her claim might not strictly be the case, she obviously feels threatened by the agency responsible for the collection of child support. In other words, in the event that lone mothers internalize the view that they are failing to self-regulate, the state in the form of the Child Support Agency is perceived as having the responsibility for ensuring conformity to acceptable standards of behaviour. Regulation is therefore exercised and experienced as an external force in addition to being experienced as an internalized phenomenon.

Women can experience both social and legal discourses in a negative manner, but there are important differences in how the power of these discourses is exercised. For example, the law on child support exercises its power through explicitly coercive and direct means targeting individual lone mothers. Social discourses, on the other hand, can and do exercise their power in a more subtle and indirect way by using negative stereotypes in order to transmit the message that lone mother headed families are undesirable and outside the norms of acceptable familial behaviour. The potential effects of the discourses also have important differences. Women can more easily resist the social discourses by distancing themselves as individuals from the stereotype of the feckless lone mother with little practical impact on their lives. However, I have argued that this strategy has the disadvantage of denying the possibility of political solidarity between women. The lone mother's resistance to legal discourse is more difficult due to the fact that the law employs coercive means in order to achieve the aim of securing women's cooperation. For example, women who refuse to cooperate with the Child Support Agency without good reason will be subjected to a benefit reduction (Child Support Act 1991, section 6). I am not saying that resistance to the law is impossible: women have refused to cooperate with the agency, and they have also resisted by ceasing to claim income support (Laws 1994: 8). But the question is then raised as to what happens to these women after they leave the benefit system? It might well be the case that women have to sacrifice a regular, though meagre, income in order to resist the law. Moreover, they may find their income reduced as a result of their failure to comply. The cost of resistance to legal discourse on child support is extremely high. The law brings punitive sanctions to bear on women who fail to comply. The effect of resisting the law is therefore potentially more threatening to the women's overall well-being than resistance to social discourse.

In this chapter, I have argued that mothers construct and negotiate their own selfhood according to behaviour deemed appropriate to meeting the needs of their children. The duty of mothers to care for their children is articulated through a discourse of realizing and meeting their children's needs. Within these discourses, a woman's own needs remain unattended to. I have revealed how women may have to provide financially for their children and for all other aspects of caring tasks. They face a number of contradictions, which must be resolved. In discourses about the needs of children, the mother's needs are occluded in two ways: by the congruence of the mother's needs with the child's; and by the translation of the mother's needs into desires, which are assigned less value than needs. Some mothers experience conflict because of wanting to work for their own personal fulfilment. However, the discourse of personal satisfaction is discredited in many discourses, for example in judicial pronouncements on residence issues.

I have also argued here that Rose understates the coercive aspects of the regulation of family life by arguing that mothers' social obligations are increasingly met by fulfilling the aspirations of their children rather than by coercive forms of regulation. I have also criticized Rose for failing to address the differences that arise between the plurality of family forms. Rose tends to speak of the idealized traditional family, for whom the concept of self-governance has greater applicability than for the marginalized family, in this case the lone mother headed family. The law on child support and the agency responsible for implementing that law rely very strongly on the threat or fear of sanction for failure to comply. Mothers often cooperate through fear of a benefit reduction, sometimes being unaware of the availability of exemption if there has been violence on the part of their estranged partner. As such, I have argued that legal discourse has a different effect from social discourse, as women who resist the law on child support can find themselves subjected to penalty for non-compliance, which could have a dramatic practical impact on their and their children's lives. The resistance to social discourse might also have a dramatic effect on the lone mother's life, though it is unlikely to have the practical effect of leaving her without sufficient funds to live. As Smart argues:

> [the] law extends itself beyond uttering the truth of law, to making claims about other areas of social life. What is important about this tendency is that the framework for such utterances remains legal – and hence retains the mantle of legal power.   (1989: 13)

The media and academic discourses discussed here contribute to the formulation of subjectivities. They also open the way for counter-discourses and various modes of resistance. While it is the case that legal discourses and their mechanisms of power can also be resisted, legal discourses can be particularly oppressive because of the way that a certain authority is ascribed to them because of their legal status. While Rose may be correct in saying that families have increasingly come to regulate themselves, his thesis has more resonances for the traditional, conforming, middle-class family. When families fail to meet the ideal, they will find themselves at the mercy of legal discourse, which still uses coercive methods to ensure that families meet their legally prescribed responsibilities.

Summary

This chapter has been concerned with revealing the ways in which the participants understand and act out their lives both within and through the discourses that constitute them. A theme that recurred throughout my discussions with the lone mothers was how they coped in the face of social, emotional and practical constraints. All the participating mothers felt stigmatized by discourses that constructed the lone mother headed household as less deserving of state support than its two-parent counterpart. They stressed that while lone mothers were represented as failing in some way, for example by not keeping a man in their lives, the expectations of lone mothers were high in that they are required to provide both financially and emotionally for their children with very little social support and encouragement.

Lone mothers cope with the stigma by stressing their abilities as mothers. They are keen to distance themselves from the negative stereotype put forward by a variety of sources. Some mothers recognize and act on a collective interest to deny that the stereotype exists. Lone mothers also strive to cope financially. The majority of women I spoke to experienced hardship as a result of their lone motherhood status. At times, limited resources meant that women often had to make personal sacrifices in order to provide for their children's needs. Women did report an increased sense of control over the whole of the family's (albeit small) income after the end of a relationship. However, the limited income that state benefits provide means that many women feel insecure and anxious about the possibility of incurring an unexpected expense that might not be covered by the income support payment and that might result in the family being thrown into debt.

Eight out of the nine participants had claimed income support at some point after the end of their relationship. Employment in the labour market was seen as the main route out of being dependent on the state for support. When asked about the problems associated with returning to work, participants cited both practical and emotional constraints. While mothers frequently articulate their motivation for work in terms of fulfilling their children's needs, it is suggested that their drive to work may also be influenced by those discourses that heap disapproval upon them for being welfare 'beneficiaries'.

Beyond conclusion: some notes for the future

At the time of writing this conclusion, media attention on the issue of child support, the lone mother headed household and the non-resident father has, to a great extent, diminished compared with the fervent press interest demonstrated in the early 1990s. However, the debate about the future of the family continues in a variety of discourses. The preceding chapters of this book drew on a number of discourses from various communities in order to show the interconnectedness and fractures both within and between discourses about the family and about the mothers and fathers that constitute families. I have examined a variety of sources, including discourses from the media, psychology, sociology, law and politics. In Chapter 1, I discussed the utility of Foucault's theory of discourse and his power/knowledge formulation for the analysis of the relationships between the law, the family, the state and society. I argued that Foucauldian discourse analysis provides a framework for examining how the power/knowledge dualism operates at the level of the micro-social order, thus providing a tool that can be utilized to analyse various sites of oppression in their particularity. I went on to identify the subject position constituted for the lone mother and examined how she is located compared with other classifications of persons, such as other mothers (for example, the valorized married mother) and the non-residential father. The adoption of theoretical analysis at the level of mundane social discourses permits a detailed examination of the new legislation on child support. The analysis of the legislation in operation aids the understanding of the specific problems encountered by different family forms both within society and before the law. The analysis of the structure and operation of the Child Support Act 1991 also demonstrates how the government, by constructing child support as a 'problem', targets mothers and fathers as the appropriate solution rather than the state. In so doing, normative guidelines are established for acceptable maternal and paternal behaviour in the post-separation context. In Chapter 2, I showed how familial groupings other than the traditional nuclear family are rendered different by social, political and legal discourse. Moreover, political rhetoric that states a preference for 'the family' also ensures that this differentiation projects a form of deviancy upon those families failing to conform to the ideal. The construction of the traditional family as the paradigmatic form serves to marginalize those groupings that may well regard themselves as families and have a right to be known as such. Women seeking to parent alone are viewed with suspicion, and indeed some fear, as they are also often blamed in part for the disintegration of 'the family'. In the same chapter, I demonstrated how the law has responded to technological developments that allow women to have children without the trappings of conventional heterosexuality. It was shown that while it is not impossible for single and lesbian women to secure licensed donor insemination, access is restricted by policy, legal regulations and practices that favour the traditional two-parent family.

Two important issues are raised about the future role of the state in supporting families in need and about the appropriate parenting roles in the post-separation context when the state is unwilling or reluctant to support families suffering financial hardship. In Chapter 3, I argued that contemporary discourses about mothering include the idea that a mother must try to ensure that her child has a father in her/his life. My analysis of disputed contact cases demonstrated how mothers who refuse paternal contact are constructed as implacably hostile. I suggest that their resistance to contact often becomes the most important factor in the case and overrides other factors, which could be more fully discussed in determining whether or not contact is in the best interests of the child. Such localized analyses bring out the fact that there is no one unified legal subject or family, that instead the law responds to shifting discourses and their constructions of the family.

While there may not be a unified legal subject, I have argued that it is possible to identify a valorized subject position against which others will be measured. For example, in Chapter 5 I examine how the perfect mother is discursively produced through discourse and how she is defined through the meeting of all her children's needs. Mothers of different class, race, ethnicity and sexuality may be judged according to how well they are perceived as meeting the child's needs as constructed from the ethnocentric, middle-class standard of the traditional Western nuclear family.

Foucault's power/knowledge combination provides a framework for understanding how some discourses are privileged over others and how those discourses to which less value is ascribed are trivialized and marginalized – as with a mother's claim to know what is best for her children. I have argued for the incorporation of an analysis of marginalized discourses into research on women's poverty, claiming that such research benefits from the inclusion of women's experience. My argument has been that questions about poverty and child support cannot be answered through restricted and restrictive debate about broad principles such as those inherent in the Child Support Act. The incorporation of women's experience provides an opportunity for marginalized discourse to take a more central position in future debates about the family, child support and mothering. The knowledge gained from the inclusion of the women's experience has utility for future governments, policy makers and legislation draftspersons who want to learn how previous family law and policy has failed lone mothers and their children and how it might be improved in the future. For example, in Chapter 5 I argued how recent policy on child support suggests that the best way for lone mothers to get off state benefit is through paid employment. Yet my discussions with lone mothers indicate that there are a number of barriers to gaining employment. Some of these can be attributed to a lack of practical support with regard to the provision of affordable childcare and help with expenses incurred as a result of taking up work outside the home, such as travel expenses. Lone mothers will also make their decision as to whether or not to go into paid employment based on a complex balance between financial and non-financial factors. Additionally, they are likely to be influenced by the common values and norms of their social group and local network.

I have also argued that mothers engage in processes of self-regulation, as described by Rose (1989) in *Governing the Soul*. In Chapter 5, I argue that lone mothers align their own personal aspirations with the happiness of their children. This idea is consonant with Rose's formulation of self-government. I have been critical of Rose for his exclusive emphasis upon the middle-class family form. His account fails to acknowledge the potential for a plurality of family forms whose experiences of normative constructions of the family may vary considerably according to their location within the network of power relations. My own work emphasizes the potential for a plurality of family forms and addresses the very particular problems that may arise for the marginalized lone mother headed household. For example, lone mothers are subjected to extreme forms of social and legal pressure to attain social and personal aspirations that are defined within a network of discourses about the idealized two-parent family. However, these constructions of the perfect family can be challenged. Discourse is therefore generative and productive and gives rise to counter-discourse, which stand as a form of resistance. However, as the final chapter demonstrated, lone mothers who resist the discourse of child support legislation may face dire consequences, possibly involving their losing their only means of income.

This book has highlighted the ways in which discourses about child support and the roles of mothers, fathers and the family as a whole have been a site and source of contestation. Lone mothers and non-residential fathers have contributed to the contemporary debates on the family and on the new child support legislation. In Chapter 4, I argued that non-residential fathers have been constructed as 'absent' in contemporary legal and social discourses about child support. The term 'absent father' used in the child support legislation connotes a number of negative ideas to do with the father being feckless, neglectful and in derogation of his paternal responsibilities. The law arrives at the idea that paternal presence is a laudable aim through the use of a diverse set of discourses that have been developed in a number of disciplines, for example sociology and the 'psy' disciplines. These views have been widely disseminated in the popular press.

Middle-class non-residential fathers have seized upon the negative constructions of the 'absent' father and have used the discourse of absence as a means of generating a counter-discourse. This opposing discourse is one that refutes the charge of absence and posits instead the real 'truth' that non-residential fathers are not really absent at all but are loving, caring fathers who happen not to reside with their children. The negative depiction of fathers is also used to demonstrate how non-residential fathers are the victims of an uncompromising and harsh government that makes it difficult for men to maintain contact with their children. Fathers' rights groups such as FNF and DAD have also sought to establish fathers as a group who are victimized by a feminism that has gone too far. Paradoxically, the negative construction of the 'absent' father has provided the non-residential father with a position of strength, with a good deal of sympathy being shown towards fathers in press discourse about child support and about the actions of the Child Support Agency in dealing with non-residential fathers. The fathers' campaign against the Child Support Act has yielded a number of radical changes to the Act that serve to benefit non-residential fathers and their second families. For example, in the Labour government's most recent White Paper on child support, 'absent' fathers become 'non-residential' fathers (HMSO 1999). The analysis of discourses on the 'absent' father has demonstrated how middle-class fathers as a group have been listened to in a way that lone mothers have not.

By identifying and explaining how men manage to use the negative representations made of them for their own ends, it becomes possible to understand how men and women are positioned at variance within the network of power relations. It also becomes clear how mothers, who are constructed as central to a child's life in terms of her providing for the child's needs, are ignored and marginalized in legal disputes over paternal contact cases.

Throughout this book, I have talked about the lone mother and *her* family in an unproblematic way, referring to the lone mother's family as constituting herself and her children. My reasons for this are that I wanted to counter those discourses that suggest that the lone mother headed family is not a real or complete family. However, it then becomes pertinent to consider how fathers fit into the family that has been fractured by separation or divorce. In Chapter 4, I outlined how fathers' groups argue that non-resident fathers are sometimes excluded from the first family after separation. When I talk of lone mothers and their families, I do not suggest that biological fathers no longer have any part in the family's life after separation or divorce.

However, I do argue in Chapter 3 that sometimes there may be good reasons to exclude a father from his child's life. The person who has primary care for the child, usually the mother, will put forward the reasons for the exclusion. I suggest that in cases where there is evidence to suggest that contact may not be in the best interests of the child, courts should not let the construction of the mother as implacably hostile to contact block consideration of other important factors in the case. I have also suggested potential reforms, based on the New Zealand system, of the current system of English law. I am arguing for an overall change in the social and legal attitude towards the lone mother headed household. Lone mothers have a legitimate claim to collective support because of the valuable work they do in raising children. At the same time, mothers who make the decision to provide the day-to-day practical care for children should not be subjected to the stigma commonly associated with state benefits. The change in attitude should recognize the importance of the care that the lone mother provides and should respond to mothers' knowledge of their children. Law and social policy should aim towards social and practical support. There should be a recognition that mothers do not make important decisions about their children's lives without a good deal of thought. It is important to have a new decoding of what lone mothers do and say in the emotional and practical activity of caring for children.

I am arguing that mothers' needs should be recognized and responded to in future social policy and legislation regarding family life. In order to ensure that mothers' needs are taken on board in future welfare programmes, it is necessary to reconceptualize the ways in which welfare issues are defined and framed. As Fraser outlines, political debates about whether or not the state should respond to social needs are typically framed in quantitative terms. Issues are raised in terms of identifying the potential needs of a given constituency, and decisions are made on the basis of what degree of help can be afforded (Fraser 1989: 145). This mode of framing is problematic for a number of reasons. First, a quantitative approach to needs issues permits only a relatively small and restricted number of answers. Second, the definition of needs is taken for granted, as if needs are self-evident and beyond dispute. As a result, there is no recognition and corresponding problematization of the concept that the construction and interpretation of people's needs is itself a political stake (*ibid.*: 145). Fraser's analysis highlights how needs are produced and interpreted through discourse. It is useful for feminism in that it elucidates the political aspects of needs interpretation. For example, in my own analysis of the government's policy on child support, I demonstrated how statistics of the rising numbers of lone mothers are cited in order to emphasize the *need* for stricter enforcement of child maintenance. In this discourse, the government raises the debate about child support in terms of a quantitative framework. The need of the government to reduce public expenditure is mapped onto the debate about the needs of lone mothers for financial support. In other words, the lone mother's need is defined as a child maintenance requirement. According to the government, the solution to the maintenance requirement is to make fathers pay. In discourses on child support, once the government has identified the need and posited the solution, further questioning of what mothers need is rendered redundant. By focusing on how needs are constructed and interpreted through discourse, it becomes possible to examine the contested and political nature of needs claims. A focus on the 'politics of need interpretation' permits an examination of the needs discourses of marginalized groups such as lone mothers (*ibid.*: 64). The extent to which the Act responds to the needs as constructed by lone mothers has been thrown into doubt by this thesis. Lone mothers' needs discourse has been silenced in contemporary social and legal debates, as has been demonstrated throughout this book. Fraser's framework permits an analysis of needs discourse that gets away from the idea that the needs of mothers are out there, readily identifiable, consonant with the political impetus of the day and solved simply by the introduction of legislation. Her emphasis is upon needs discourse as a site of contestation. Her project is concerned with revealing the conditions of possibility for developing emancipatory ways of talking about needs discourse. It takes the debate beyond the idea that social needs are simply out there, readily identifiable and beyond contestation.

This book has examined some of the discourses that constitute the 'problem' of child support and construct the roles of 'the family', lone mothers and non-residential fathers. I have sought to demonstrate the importance of reading and re-reading the legal discourse and social discourse that map out what it means to be a mother and a father in contemporary Western society in the post-separation context. I have revealed the mercurial and diverse constructions of mothers and fathers in social and legal discourses. It has been my concern to fracture the idea that there is a unified and stable family of law. I am willing to enter into current and future debates about the future of the family, but I reject the idea that the debate should be framed around how best to reinstate the traditional family of some mythical golden age. Rather, I seek to direct the route of reform to rewriting family policy and law to accommodate the changes in family structure. I also use the term 'reform' in the sense of wanting to change attitudes towards families who do not desire or cannot achieve the traditional family form but who may still want a family to call their own.

bibliography

Abbott, D. (1994) 'Child support and clean break: once a parent . . .', *New Law Journal*, 18 Feb.

Allen, H. (1987) *Justice Unbalanced*. Milton Keynes: Open University Press.

Arnup, K. (1989) ' "Mothers just like others;" lesbians, divorce and child custody in Canada', *Canadian Journal of Women and the Law* 3 (1): 18–32.

Arnup, K. (1994) 'Finding fathers: artificial insemination, lesbians and the law', *Canadian Journal of Welfare Law* 7 (1): 97–115.

Bailey, M.E. (1993) 'Foucauldian feminism: Contesting bodies, sexuality and identity', in Ramazonoglu, C. (ed.) *Up Against Foucault: Explorations of Some Tensions Between Foucault and Feminism*. London: Routledge.

Bainham, A. and Cretney, S. (1993) *Children: The Modern Law*. Bristol: Jordan Publishing.

Barnett, A. (1999) 'Disclosure of domestic violence by women involved in child contact disputes', *Family Law* 104–7.

Beail, N. and McGuire, J. (eds) (1982) *Fathers: Psychological Perspectives*. London: Junction Books.

Beck, U. (1992) *Risk Society: Towards a New Modernity*. London: Sage.

Bell, C. and Roberts, H. (eds) (1984) *Social Researching: Politics, Problems, Practice*. London: Routledge & Kegan Paul.

Bell, V. (1993) *Interrogating Incest: Feminism, Foucault and Law*. London: Routledge.

Beresford, S. (1994) 'Lesbian mothers in custody cases', *Family Law* 24: 643–5.

Berry, P. (ed.) (1990) *Fathers and Mothers*. Dallas, Texas: Spring Publications.

Biller, H.B. (1971) *Father, Child and Sex Role: Paternal Determinants of Personality Development*. Lexington: Heath.

Blunkett, D. (1999) *Brown and Blunkett Put Children and the Family First*. London: Department of Education and Employment http://193.32.28.101/coi/coipress 1–8.

Bly, R. (1990) 'The hunger for the king in a time with no father', in Berry, P. (ed.) *Fathers and Mothers*. Dallas, Texas: Spring Publications.

Bombyk, M., Bricker-Jenkins, M. and Wedenoja, M. (1985) 'Reclaiming our profession through feminist research: some methodological issues in the feminist practice project', in Kourany, J.A., Sterba, J.P. and Tong, R. (eds) *Feminist Philosophies*. Hemel Hempstead: Harvester Wheatsheaf.

Bordo, S. (1990) 'Reading the slender body', in Jacobus, M., Fox Keller, E. and Shuttleworth, S. (eds) *Body/Politics: Women and the Discourses of Science*. London: Routledge.

Bowlby, J. (1951) *Maternal Care and Mental Health*. Geneva: World Health Organisation.

Boyd, S. (1992) 'What is a "normal" family?' *Modern Law Review* 55: 269–78.

Boyd, S. (1996) 'Is there an ideology of motherhood in (post)modern child custody law?' *Social and Legal Studies* 5 (4): 495–521.

Brannen, J. and Wilson, G. (eds) (1987) *Give and Take in Families: Studies in Resource Distribution*. London: Allen & Unwin.

Bristow, A. and Esper, J. (1988) 'A feminist research ethos', in Nebraska Sociological Feminist Collective (ed.) *A Feminist Ethic for Social Science Research*. New York: Edwin Mellen Press.

Brophy, J. (1985) 'Child care and the growth of power: the status of mothers in child custody disputes', in Brophy, J. and Smart, C. (eds) *Women in Law: Explorations in Law, Family and Sexuality*. London: Routledge & Kegan Paul.

Brophy, J. and Smart, C. (eds) (1985) *Women in Law: Explorations in Law, Family and Sexuality*. London: Routledge & Kegan Paul.

Brown, J. (1989) *Why Don't They Go to Work? Mothers on Benefit*, SSAC Research Paper No. 2. London: HMSO.

Bryson, A. and Rowlingson, K. (1994) *Hard Times? How Poor Families Make Ends Meet*. London: Policy Studies Institute.

Butler, J. (1990) *Gender Trouble: Feminism and the Subversion of Identity*. London: Routledge.

Campbell, B. (1993) *Goliath: Britain's Dangerous Places*. London: Methuen.

Chandler, J. (1991) *Women Without Husbands: An Exploration of the Margins of Marriage*. London: Macmillan.

Chapman, R. and Rutherford, J. (eds) (1988) *Male Order: Unwrapping Masculinity*. London: Lawrence & Wishart.

Chodorow, N. (1978) *The Reproduction of Mothering*. Berkeley: University of California Press.

Collier, R. (1992) ' "The art of living the married life": representations of male heterosexuality in law', *Social and Legal Studies* 1: 543–63.

Collier, R. (1995a) *Masculinity, Law and the Family*. London: Routledge.

Collier, R. (1995b) ' "Waiting till father gets home . . .": family values and the reconstruction of fatherhood in family law', *Social and Legal Studies* 4 (1): 1–30.

Collier, R. (1998) *Masculinities, Crime and Criminology*. London: Sage.

Cooper, D. and Herman, D. (1991) 'Getting "the family right": legislating heterosexuality in Britain 1986–1991', *Canadian Journal of Family Law* 10: 41–78.

Crane, P. (1982) *Gays and the Law*. London: Pluto.

Daly, M. (1978) *Gyn/Ecology: The Metaethics of Radical Feminism*. Boston: Beacon Press.

Davis, G. and Pearce, J. (1999) 'On the trail of the welfare principle', *Family Law* 144–8.

Dennis, N. and Erdos, G. (1992) *Families Without Fatherhood*. London: Institute of Economic Affairs.

Department of Social Security (1994) *Proposed Changes to Child Support Maintenance*. London: HMSO.

Diamond, I. and Quinby, L. (eds) (1988) *Foucault & Feminism: Reflections on Resistance*. Boston: Northeastern University Press.

Diduck, A. (1995) 'The unmodified family: the Child Support Act and the construction of legal subjects', *Journal of Law and Society* 22 (4): 527–48.

Diduck, A. and Kaganas, F. (1999) *Family Law, Gender and the State: Text, Cases and Materials*. Oxford: Hart Publishing.

Dilnot, A. and Walker, I. (eds) (1989) *The Economics of Social Security*. Oxford: Oxford University Press.

Dobash, R. and Dobash, R.P. (1970) *Violence Against Wives*. London: Free Press.

Donzelot, J. (1980) *The Policing of Families*. London: Hutchinson.

Douglas, G. (1990) 'Family law under the Thatcher government', *Journal of Law and Society* 17 (4): 411–26.

Douglas, G. (1992) *Law, Fertility and Reproduction*. London: Sweet & Maxwell.

Duskin, E. (ed.) (1990) *Lone-Parent Families: The Economic Challenge*. London: HMSO.

Edwards, R. and Duncan, S. (1996) 'Rational economic man or lone mothers in cotext? The uptake of paid work', in Silva, E.B. (ed.) *Good Enough Mothering? Feminist Perspectives on Lone Motherhood*. London: Routledge 114–29.

Edwards, S. and Halpern, A. (1992) 'Parental responsibility: and instrument of social policy' *Family Law* 22: 113–18.

Eekelaar, J. (1991) 'Parental responsibility: state of nature or nature of the state?', *Journal of Social Welfare and Family Law* 13: 37–50.

Eekelaar, J. (1994) 'Third thoughts on child support', *Family Law* 24: 99–102.

Eekelaar, J. and Maclean, M. (1986) *Maintenance After Divorce*. Oxford: Clarendon Press.

ESRC (1992) *Income Security in Britain: A Research and Policy Agenda for the Next Ten Years*. London: ESRC.

Etzioni, A. (1993) *The Parenting Deficit*. London: Demos.

Finch, J. (1984) ' "It's great to have someone to talk to": the ethics and politics of interviewing women', in Bell, C. and Roberts, H. (eds) *Social Researching: Politics, Problems, Practice*. London: Routledge & Kegan Paul.

Finch, J. (1992) 'State responsibility and family responsibility for financial support in the 1990's', in *Income Security in Britain: A Research and Policy Agenda for the Next Ten Years*. London: ESRC.

Finch, J. (1996) 'Women, "the" family and families', in Cosslett, T., Easton, A. and Summerfield, P. (eds) *Women, Power and Resistance: An Introduction to Women's Studies*. Buckingham: Open University Press, 13–22.

Fineman, M. (1992) 'The neutered mother', *University of Miami Law Review* 46: 653–69.

Fineman, M. (1995) *The Neutered Mother, the Sexual Family and Other Twentieth Century Tragedies*. London: Routledge.

Finer, M. and McGregor, O.R. (1974) 'The history of the obligation to maintain', *Report of the Committee on One-Parent Families* (Cmnd 5629-1) (appendices) 2. London: HMSO.

Finlayson, L. and Marsh, A. (1998) 'Lone parents on the margins of work', in Ford, R. and Millar, J. (eds) *Private Lives & Public Responses: Lone Parenthood & Future Policy in the UK*. London: Policy Studies Institute, 193–207.

Ford, R. (1998) 'Lone mothers' decisions whether or not to work', in Ford, R. and Millar, J. (eds) *Private Lives & Public Responses: Lone Parenthood & Future Policy in the UK*. London: Policy Studies Institute, 208–25.

Ford, R. and Millar, J. (1998) 'Lone parenthood in the UK: policy dilemmas and solutions', in Ford, R. and Millar, J. (eds) *Private Lives & Public Responses: Lone Parenthood & Future Policy in the UK*. London: Policy Studies Institute, 1–21.

Foucault, M. (1976) 'Two lectures', in Gordon, C. (ed. and trans.) (1980) *Power/Knowledge*. Hemel Hempstead: Harvester Wheatsheaf.

Foucault, M. (1977) *Discipline and Punish* (A. Sheridan trans.). Harmondsworth: Peregrine.

Foucault, M. (1980) 'The eye of power', in Gordon, C. (ed. and trans.) (1980) *Power/Knowledge*. Hemel Hempstead: Harvester Wheatsheaf.

Foucault, M. (1981) *History of Sexuality*, Vol. 1 (R. Hurley trans.). London: Penguin.

Francis, S. and James, S. (1993) *Dossier of DSS Illegalities: Implications of the Child Support Act*. London: Campaign Against the Child Support Act.

Fraser, N. (1989) *Unruly Practices: Power, Discourse and Gender in Contemporary Social Theory*. Cambridge: Polity Press.

Fraser, N. and Nicholson, L.J. (1990) 'Social criticism without philosophy: an encounter between feminism and postmodernism', in Nicholson, L.J. (ed.) *Feminism/Postmodernism*. London: Routledge.

George, V. and Miller, S. (1994) *Social Policy Towards 2000: Squaring the Welfare Circle*. London: Routledge.

Gibson, C. (1994) *Dissolving Wedlock*. London: Routledge.

Glendinning, C. and Millar, J. (eds) (1992) *Women and Poverty in Britain, the 1990s*. Hemel Hempstead: Harvester Wheatsheaf.

Glenn, E.N., Chang, G. and Forcey, L.R. (eds) (1994) *Mothering: Ideology, Experience and Agency*. London: Routledge.

Gordon, C. (ed. and trans.) (1980) *Power/Knowledge*. Hemel Hempstead: Harvester Wheatsheaf.

Graham, H. (1984) 'Surveying through stories', in Bell, C. and Roberts, H. (eds) *Social Researching: Politics, Problems, Practice*. London: Routledge & Kegan Paul.

Graham, H. (1987) 'Being poor: perceptions and coping strategies of lone mothers', in Brannen, J. and Wilson, G. (eds) *Give and Take in Families: Studies in Resource Distribution*. London: Allen & Unwin.

Graycar, R. (1989) 'Equal rights *Versus* fathers' rights', in Smart, C. and Sevenhuijsen, S. (eds) *Child Custody and the Politics of Gender*. London: Routledge.

Gregory, I. (1965) 'Anterospective data following childhood loss of a parent', *Arch. gen. Psychiat*. 13: 99–109.

Hartsock, N. (1990) 'Foucault on power: a theory for women', in Nicholson, L.J. (ed.) *Feminism/Postmodernism*. London: Routledge.

Hearn, J. (1987) *The Gender of Oppression: Men, Masculinity and the Critique of Marxism*. Sussex: Wheatsheaf Books.

Heelas, P. and Morris, P. (1992) *The Values of the Enterprising Culture*. London: Routledge.

Hester, M. and Radford, J. (1996) 'Contradictions and compromises: the impact of the Children Act on women and children's safety', in Hester, M., Kelly, L. and Radford, J. (eds) *Women, Violence and Male Power: Feminist Activism, Research and Practice*. Buckingham: Open University Press.

Hester, M., Kelly, L. and Radford, J. (eds) (1996) *Women, Violence and Male Power: Feminist Activism, Research and Practice*. Open University Press: Buckingham.

Hewitt, P. and Leach, P. (1993) *Social Justice, Children and Families*. London: Institute for Public Policy Research.

HMSO (1985) *Reform of Social Security: Programme for Action* (Cmnd 9691). London: HMSO.

HMSO (1990) *Children Come First, The Government's Proposals on the Maintenance of Children* (Cmnd 1264) 2. London: HMSO.

HMSO (1991) *Social Trends*. A publication of the Government Statistical Service. London: HMSO.

HMSO (1995) *Improving Child Support* (Cmnd 2745). London: HMSO.

HMSO (1998) *Children First: A New Approach to Child Support* (Cmnd 3992). London: HMSO.

HMSO (1999) *A New Contract for Welfare: Children's Rights and Parents' Responsibilities*: http://www.dss.gov.uk/hq/pubs/childsup/main/chpt3.htm

hooks, B. (1993) 'Sisterhood: political solidarity between women', in Kourany, J.A., Sterba, J.P. and Tong, R. (eds) *Feminist Philosophies*. Hemel Hempstead: Harvester Wheatsheaf.

Horrocks, R. (1994) *Masculinity in Crisis: Myths, Fantasies and Realities*. London: Macmillan.

Ingman, T. (1996) 'Contact and the obdurate parent', *Family Law* 615.

Irigaray, L. (1993) *je, tu, nous: Toward a Culture of Difference*. London: Routledge.

Irigaray, L. (1987) 'Is the subject of science sexed?' Carol Mastrangelo Bove (trans.), *Hypatia* 2 (3): 65–87.

Irvine, Lord (1999) *£3 Million for Marriage Support*. London: Lord Chancellor's Department. http://193.32.28.101/coi/coipress 1–2.

Jacobus, M., Fox Keller, E. and Shuttleworth, S. (eds) (1990) *Body/Politics: Women and the Discourses of Science*. London: Routledge.

James, A. and Prout, A. (eds) (1990) *Constructing and Reconstructing Childhood*. London: Falmer Press.

Joshi, H. (1990) 'Obstacles and opportunities for lone parents as breadwinners in Great Britain', in Duskin, E. (ed.) *Lone-Parent Families: The Economic Challenge*. Organisation for Economic Co-operation and Development (OECD), London: HMSO.

Kaganas, F. (1999) 'Contact, conflict and risk', in Day Sclater, S. and Piper, C. (eds) *Undercurrents of Divorce*. Aldershot: Ashgate.

Katz Rothman, B. (1994) 'Beyond mothers and fathers: ideology in a patriarchal society', in Glenn, E.N., Chang, G. and Forcey, L.R. (eds) *Mothering: Ideology, Experience and Agency*. London: Routledge.

Kaufman, M. (ed.) (1987) *Beyond Patriarchy: Essays by Men on Pleasure, Power and Change*. Toronto: Oxford University Press.

Kelly, L. (1988) *Surviving Sexual Violence*. Cambridge: Polity Press.

King, M. (1987) 'Playing the symbols – custody and the Law Commission', *Family Law* 186.

King, M. and Piper, C. (1990) *How the Law Thinks about Children*. Aldershot: Gower.

Kourany, J.A., Sterba, J.P. and Tong, R. (eds) (1993) *Feminist Philosophies*. Hemel Hempstead: Harvester Wheatsheaf.

Law Commission (1982) *Family Law: Illegitimacy*. Law Com, No. 118. London: HMSO.

Lawler, S. (1995) *Mothering the Self: A Study of the Mother–Daughter Relationship*. Lancaster: Lancaster University.

Laws, S. (1994) 'Un-Valued Families', *Trouble & Strife* 28: 5–11.

Lewis, C. (1982) 'The observation of father–infant relationships: an "attachment" to outmoded concepts', in McKee, L. and O'Brien, M. (eds) *The Father Figure: Some Current Orientations and Historical Perspectives*. London: Tavistock.

Lewis, C. and O'Brien, M. (eds) (1987) *Reassessing Fatherhood*. London: Sage.

Lewis, J. (1998) 'The problem of lone-mother families in twentieth-century Britain', *Journal of Social Welfare and Family Law* 20 (3): 251–83.

Lewis, J. and Piachaud, D. (1992) 'Women and poverty in the twentieth century', in Glendinning, C. and Millar, J. *Women and Poverty in Britain, the 1990s*. Hemel Hempstead: Wheatsheaf.

Lidington, B. (1992) *A New Tax on the Children of Divorce*. London: Families Need Fathers.

Lister, R. (1989) 'Assessment of the Fowler Review', in Dilnot, A. and Walker, I. (eds) *The Economics of Social Security*. Oxford: Oxford University Press.

Lister, R. (1992) in Glendinning, C. and Millar, J. *Women and Poverty in Britain, the 1990s*. Hemel Hempstead: Wheatsheaf.

Lochhead, L. (1984) 'Everybody's Mother', in Dawson, J. (ed.) (1992) *The Virago Book of Wicked Verse*, London: Virago, 135. Originally in *Dreaming Frankenstein and Collected Poems*, London: Polygon.

Maclean, S. and Eekelaar, J. (1987) *The Parental Obligation*. Oxford: Hart Publishing.

Maidment, S. (1984) *Child Custody and Divorce*. London: Croom Helm.

Maidment, S. (1998) 'Parental alienation syndrome – a judicial response?' *Family Law* 264–5.

McCall-Smith, A. (1990) 'Is anything left of parental rights?' in McCall-Smith, A. and Sutherland, A. (eds) *Family Rights*. Edinburgh: Edinburgh University Press.

McCall-Smith, A. and Sutherland, A. (eds) (1990) *Family Rights*. Edinburgh: Edinburgh University Press.

McKee, L. and O'Brien, M. (1982) *The Father Figure: Some Current Orientations and Historical Perspectives*. London: Tavistock.

McNeil, M. (1993) 'Dancing with Foucault: feminism and power–knowledge', in Ramazonoglu, C. (ed.) *Up Against Foucault: Explorations of Some Tensions Between Foucault and Feminism*. London: Routledge.

Metcalf, A. and Humphries, M. (1985) *The Sexuality of Men*. London: Pluto Press.

Millar, J. (1994) 'State, family and personal responsibility: the changing balance for lone mother in the United Kingdom', *Feminist Review* 48: 24–39.

Mnookin, R.H. (1975) 'Child custody adjudication: judicial functions in the face of indeterminacy', *Law and Contemporary Problems* 39 (3): 226–93.

Mostyn, N. (1999) 'The Green Paper on child support – Children First: a new approach to child support', *Family Law* 29: 95–103.

Muraro, L. (1993) 'More women Than men', in Irigaray, L. *je, tu, nous: Toward a Culture of Difference*. London: Routledge.

NAB (1954) *The National Assistance Board's Annual Report* (19 Cmnd 9210). London: HMSO.

National Council for One Parent Families (1990) *Barriers to Work: A Study of Lone Parents' Training and Employment Needs*. London: NCOPF.

National Council for One Parent Families (1993) *Key Facts*. London: NCOPF.

National Council for One Parent Families (1994) *Key Facts*. London: NCOPF.

National Council for One Parent Families (1994–95) *Annual Report*. London: NCOPF.

Neale, B. and Smart, C. (1995) *The New Parenthood? Discussions from the ESRC Project 'The Legal and Moral Ordering of Households in Transition'*. Leeds: GAPU Sociology and Social Policy Research Working Paper 13.

Neale, B. and Smart, C. (1999) *Family Fragments?* Cambridge: Polity Press.

Nicholson, L.J. (ed.) (1990) *Feminism/Postmodernism*. London: Routledge.

O'Brien, M. (1982) 'The Working Father', in Beail, N. and McGuire, J. (eds) *Fathers: Psychological Perspectives*. London: Junction Books.

O'Donovan, K. (1993) *Family Law Matters*. London: Pluto Press.

Oakley, A. (1985) *The Sociology of Housework*. Oxford: Basil Blackwell.

Oakley, A. (1972) *Sex, Gender and Society*. London: Temple Smith.

Oakley, A. (1981) 'Interviewing women: a contradiction in terms', in Roberts, H. (ed.) *Doing Feminist Research*. London: Routledge & Kegan Paul.

Oppenheim, C. and Harker, L. (1996) *Poverty: The Facts*, 3rd edn. London: Child Poverty Action Group.

Pahl, J. (1983) 'The allocation of money and the structuring of inequality within marriage', *Sociological Review* 31: 237–62.

Phelan, S. (1990) 'Foucault and feminism', *American Journal of Political Science* 34 (2): 421–40.

Pogrebin, L. (1981) *Growing Up Free*. New York: McGraw-Hill.

Probyn, E. (1993) *Sexing the Self: Gendered Positions in Cultural Studies*. London: Routledge.

Radford, J. (1996) ' "Nothing really happened": the invalidation of women's experiences of sexual violence', in Hester, M., Kelly, L. and Radford, J. (eds) *Women, Violence and Male Power: Feminist Activism, Research and Practive*. Buckingham: Open University Press.

Ramazonoglu, C. (ed.) (1993) *Up Against Foucault: Explorations of Some Tensions Between Foucault and Feminism*. London: Routledge.

Ransom, J. (1993) 'Feminism, difference and discourse: the limits of discursive analysis for feminism', in Ramazonoglu, C. (ed.) *Up Against Foucault: Explorations of Some Tensions Between Foucault and Feminism*. London: Routledge.

Reece, H. (1996) 'The paramountcy principle: consensus or construct?' *Current Legal Problems* 49: 267–304.

Reinharz, S. (1992) *Feminist Methods in Social Research*. New York: Oxford University Press.

Robertson Elliot, F. (1989) 'The family: private arena or adjunct of the state?', *Journal of Law and Society* 16 (4): 443–63.

Robinson, M. (1991) *Family Transformations through Divorce and Remarriage*. London: Routledge.

Rosaldo, M. (1974) 'Woman, culture and society: a theoretical overview', in Rosaldo, M. and Lamphere, L. (eds) *Woman, Culture and Society*. Stanford, California: Stanford University Press.

Rosaldo, M. and Lamphere, L. (eds) (1974) *Woman, Culture and Society*. Stanford, California: Stanford University Press.

Rose, N. (1987) 'Transcending the public/private', *Journal of Law and Society* 14 (1): 61–76.

Rose, N. (1989) *Governing the Soul: The Shaping of the Private Self*. London: Routledge.

Rose, N. (1992) 'Governing the enterprising self', in Heelas, P. and Morris, P. (eds) *The Values of the Enterprising Culture*. London: Routledge.

Rotundo, E.A. (1987) 'Patriarchs and participants: a historical perspective on fatherhood in the United States', in Kaufman, M. (ed.) *Beyond Patriarchy: Essays by Men on Pleasure, Power and Change*. Toronto: Oxford University Press.

Rutter, M. (1966) *Children of Sick Parents: An Environmental and Psychiatric Study*. Oxford: Oxford University Press.

Rutter, M. (1972) *Maternal Deprivation Reassessed*. London: Penguin.

Segal, L. (1990) *Slow Motion: Changing Masculinities, Changing Men*. London: Virago.

Seidler, V. (1985) 'Fear and intimacy', in Metcalf, A. and Humphries, M. (eds) *The Sexuality of Men*. London: Pluto Press.

Seidler, V. (1988) 'Fathering, authority and masculinity', in Chapman, R. and Rutherford, J. (eds) *Unwrapping Masculinity*. London: Lawrence & Wishart.

Seidler, V. (1994) *Unreasonable Men: Masculinity and Social Theory*. London: Routledge.

SFLA and FLBA (1993) 'The Child Support Act – policies for reform', *Family Law* 23: 700–2.

Smart, C. (1987) ' "There is of course the distinction dictated by nature": law and the problem of paternity', in Stanworth, M. (ed.) *Reproductive Technologies: Gender, Motherhood and Medicien*. Minneapolis: University of Minnesota Press.

Smart, C. (1989) *Feminism and the Power of Law*. London: Routledge.

Smart, C. (1991) 'The legal and moral ordering of child custody', *Journal of Law and Society* 18 (4): 485–500.

Smart, C. (1992) 'Disruptive bodies and unruly sex: the regulation of reproduction and sexuality in the nineteenth century', in Smart, C. (ed.) *Regulating Womanhood: Historical Essays on Marriage, Motherhood and Sexuality*. London: Routledge.

Smart, C. (1995) 'The family and social change', in Neale, B. and Smart, C. *The New Parenthood? Discussions from the ESRC Project 'The Legal and Moral Ordering of*

Households in Transition'. Leeds: GAPU Sociology and Social Policy Research Working Paper 13.

Smart, C. and Neale, B. (1999) *Family Fragments?* Cambridge: Polity Press.

Smart, C. and Sevenhuijsen, S. (eds) (1989) *Child Custody and the Politics of Gender*. London: Routledge.

Snowden, R. and Mitchell, G. (1981) *The Artificial Family: A Consideration of Artificial Insemination by Donor*. London: Unwin Paperbacks.

Social Security Committee (1994) *The Operation of the Child Support Act* (Fifth Report), Session 1993–94. London: HMSO.

Spelman, E. and Lugones M. (1993) 'Have we got a theory for you! Feminist theory, cultural imperialism and the demand for "the woman's voice"', in Kourany, J.A., Sterba, J.P. and Tong, R. (eds) *Feminist Philosophies*. Hemel Hempstead: Harvester Wheatsheaf.

Spensky, M. (1992) 'Producers of legitimacy: Homes for unmarried mothers in the 1950's', in Smart, C. (ed.) *Regulating Womanhood: Historical Essays on Marriage, Motherhood and Sexuality*. London: Routledge.

Stanworth, M. (ed.) (1987) *Reproductive Technologies: Gender, Motherhood and Medicine*. Minneapolis: University of Minnesota Press.

Tronto, J. (1993) *Moral Boundaries: A Political Argument for an Ethic of Care*. London: Routledge.

Vogler, C. (1989) *Labour Market Change and Patterns of Financial Allocation Within Households*. Oxford: ESRC/Social Change and Economic Life Initiative, Working Paper No. 12.

Walker, C. (1993) *Managing Poverty: The Limits of Social Assistance*. London: Routledge.

Walkerdine, V. and Lucey, H. (1989) *Democracy in the Kitchen: Regulating Mothers and Socialising Daughters*. London: Virago.

Wallbank, J. (1997) 'The campaign for change of the Child Support Act 1991: Reconstituting the "absent" father'. *Social and Legal Studies* 6 (2): 191–216.

Wandor, M. (ed.) (1972) *The Body Politic: Women's Liberation in Britain 1969–1972*. London: Stage One.

Warner, M. (1994) *Six Myths of Our Time: Managing Monsters*, the Reith Lectures. London: Vintage.

Warnock, M. (1985) *A Question of Life: The Warnock Report on Human Fertilisation and Embryology*. Oxford: Basil Blackwell.

Weedon, C. (1987) *Feminist Practice and Poststructuralist Theory*. Oxford: Basil Blackwell.

Winnicott, D.W. (1965a) 'The development of the capacity for concern', in Winnicott, D.W. (ed.) *Maturational Processes and the Facilitating Environment*. New York: International Universities Press.

Winnicott, D.W. (1965b) *The Maturational Processes and the Facilitating Environment*. New York: International Universities Press.

Woodhead, M. (1990) 'Psychology and the cultural construction of children's needs', in James, A. and Prout, A. (eds) *Constructing and Reconstructing Childhood*. London: Falmer Press.

Wortis, R. (1972) 'Child-rearing and women's liberation', in Wandor, M. (ed.) *The Body Politic: Women's Liberation in Britain 1969–1972*. London: Stage One.

Young, A. (1996) *Imagining Crime*. London: Sage.

Young, I.M. (ed.) (1990) *Throwing Like a Girl and Other Essays in Feminist Philosophy and Social Theory*. Bloomington and Indianapolis: Indiana University Press.

Newspapers

Daily Mail.

Daily Telegraph.

The Guardian.

The Independent.

The Independent on Sunday.

The Observer.

The Times.

Cases

Crozier *v.* Crozier [1994] 2 All ER 362.

C *v.* S [1987] 1 All ER 1230.

Delaney *v.* Delaney [1990] 2 FLR 457.

Harrington *v.* Hynes, [1982] 8 Family Law Reports (Australia) 295–76.

K *v.* K (Minors: Property Transfer) [1992] 2 FLR 220 CA.

Paton *v.* British Pregnancy Advisory Service Trustees [1979] QB 276.

Re H (Minors) (Access) [1992] 1 FLR 148.

Re J (A Minor) (Contact) [1994] 1 FLR 729.

Re O (Contact: Impositions of Conditions) [1995] 2 FLR 124.

Re P (A Minor) (Contact) [1994] 2 FLR 374.

Re P (Contact) (Supervision) [1996] 2 FLR 314.

Re R (Contact: Consent Order) [1995] 1 FLR.

Re W (A Minor) (Contact) [1994] 2 FLR 441.

Tyler *v.* Tyler [1989] 2 FLR 158.

Statutes

Child Support Act 1991.

Child Support Act 1995.

Children Act 1989.

Children and Young Person's Act 1933.

Criminal Justice Act 1991.

Guardianship Amendment Act 1995.

Guardianship of Minors' Act 1925.

Housing Act 1996.

Human Fertilisation and Embryology Act 1990.

Local Government Act 1988.

Matrimonial and Family Proceedings Act 1984.

Matrimonial Causes Act 1973.

Miscellaneous material

Child Support (Information, Evidence and Disclosure) Regulations 1992, SI 1992/ 1812.

Child Support (Maintenance Assessment Procedure) Regulations 1992, SI 1992/ 1813.

Code of Practice, Human Fertilisation and Embryology Authority, s. 3.16(b).

CSAReg 1(2) CS(MASC) Regs as amended by Reg 40(2)(a) CS(MA)2 Regs.

Families Need Fathers, charity pamphlet.

Hansard, Vol. 981. Col. 1463, 26 March 1980.

Hansard, Vol. 192, 1990–91.

Lord Chancellor's Advisory Board on Family Law (Children Act Sub-Committee) (1999) *Contact Between Children and Violent Parents: Further Consultation Paper on the Question of Parental Contact with Children in Cases where there is Domestic Violence.* London: Lord Chancellor's Department.

Parliamentary Debates, *Special Standing Committee, Matrimonial and Family Proceedings Bill* 20, London.

The Pink Paper.

Schedule 1, para. 4 to the 1991 Act; the Child Support (Maintenance Assessment and Special Cases) Regulations 1992, SI 1992/1815, Reg. 6.

Schedule 1, para. 7 (1) to the 1991 Act; the Child Support (Maintenance Assessments and Special Cases) Regulations 1992, SI 1992/1815, Reg. 13.

Social Security (Child Maintenance *Bonus*) Regs, SI 1996/3195.

Wages for Housework campaign and Payday men's network (1993) *Against Redistributing Poverty: Counting the Cost to Women, Children and Men of the State's Child Maintenance Plan.* Centrepiece: London.

index